(continued from front flap)

Parts of this book have already been used in a number of disciplines. A part was introduced into a training seminar for psychiatric residents and proved an excellent springboard for discussion of different approaches to understanding young children's behavior. It has also been a teaching tool in the supervision of Special Education teachers and social workers. And it has been used effectively with New York City vocational high school students who expect to become paraprofessionals working with children.

Phyllis Brusiloff is presently organizer of a Therapeutic Nursery Group in a day-care center of the Child Development Center, Jewish Board of Guardians. She has lectured at Anna Freud's Hampstead Clinic and is Principal Investigator under an N.I.M.H. grant to train nursery school teachers in therapeutic intervention with preschool children. Mary Jane Witenberg is Director and Teacher-Therapist of the Therapeutic Program at the Hudson Guild Counseling Service and consultant to St. Luke's Hospital Therapeutic Nursery.

*The
Emerging
Child*

PHYLLIS BRUSILOFF
MARY JANE WITENBERG

The
Emerging
Child

With an Introduction by CLARICE KESTENBAUM, M.D.

JASON ARONSON, PUBLISHER

To Sherman O. Schachter
with deepest gratitude
and to our families
for their love and encouragement.

Library of Congress Catalog Card Number: 72-94352
ISBN: 0–87668–063–5
Manufactured in the United States of America

Mary Jane Witenberg died suddenly the day before the galleys of The Emerging Child *arrived. Our collaboration was a rich and satisfying experience; and this volume is the fruition of her years of experience. Those who knew her will find her again on these pages. Those who never knew her will find her interest, dedication and knowledge of young troubled children a source of inspiration.*

Phyllis Brusiloff
September 1973

Contents

Preface

TUCKED AWAY in the inner city of New York is a small, unique* therapeutic nursery program. It is maintained with moderate expenditure and can easily be duplicated in any nursery or day care center.

The Hudson Guild is a long-established neighborhood house which offers social, educational, psychiatric, and psychological services to the residents of Chelsea, who are often socially, economically, and educationally deprived. The many activities of the Hudson Guild

---

*There are therapeutic nursery programs in hospital settings and in treatment facilities. At the time Hudson Guild's TNG was established, there was no duplication of the program, as far as we know, within any kind of normal preschool program. Subsequently, based on the prototype of the Hudson Guild's TNG, Phyllis Brusiloff established a similar program at Goddard–Riverside Day Care Center under the auspices of the Child Development Center.

Neighborhood House include a mental hygiene clinic, also called the Counseling Service, and the operation of a day care center for the children of working mothers. Dr. David Wolitzky describes the program: "In 1956 the staffs of these two independent services embarked on a cooperative continuing venture—the establishment and operation of the Therapeutic Nursery Group (TNG). The aim of TNG is to provide emotionally and behaviorally disturbed preschool children with a group–play therapy experience under the leadership of a special nursery group teacher–therapist. The basic rationale of this program is that the early detection and treatment of psychological disturbances serves as a constructive influence on the child's current and subsequent personal and social adaptation. The clinical evidence of the personnel involved in this program is that the TNG, in providing a corrective emotional experience, is an effective mode of intervention." This book presents the background, nature, techniques, and implications of the TNG program.

The children's response to this unusual form of treatment generates enthusiasm and excitement. We hope that the understanding and techniques that have evolved from our experiences as teacher–therapists in this unique treatment facility will be useful and open the door to many imaginative alternatives in working with young children in a TNG or in a nursery room.

Acknowledgments

NUMEROUS PEOPLE have made important contributions to the development and continued operation of the Therapeutic Nursery Groups at the Hudson Guild's Mental Hygiene Clinic. We are deeply indebted to Dr. Margaret Mahler who, with the late Ann Lambert, played a primary role in the formation of the first Therapeutic Nursery Group in 1956 by setting forth guiding philosophical and therapeutic principles.

We are grateful to Mrs. Frances Schoor, the first teacher–therapist who implemented, with skill and talent, these principles which have continued to serve as a concrete model for the training and therapeutic work of subsequent teacher–therapists.

The other members of the original staff who helped

launch the Therapeutic Nursery Group program were Virginia Moore, M.D., Fred Pine, Ph.D., S. R. Slavson, Evelyn Stiefel, M.S.W., Paula Balzer, M.S.W., and the directors of the Hudson Guild's Day Care Center, Mrs. Gladys Reisser and Mrs. Marion Easton.

The continued operation of the Therapeutic Nursery Group has always depended upon the eager cooperation of the Hudson Guild's Mental Hygiene Clinic. The consultants and staff of this counseling service have participated creatively in many aspects of the Therapeutic Nursery Group program in the form of therapeutic supervision, psychological testing, research evaluation, and contacts with the parents of the Therapeutic Nursery Group children.

Mr. Jack Sasaki, M.S.W., the administrator of the Mental Hygiene Clinic, has given our work constant support and encouragement. The interest and contributions of the medical directors, Sherman O. Schachter, M.D., and Harvey Rosenblatt, M.D., are deeply appreciated.

The Hudson Guild Day Care Center staff has assisted in the operation of the Therapeutic Nursery Group. Marion Easton, director, and the staff of hard–working, involved teachers furthered the aims of the program. We appreciate the help of the Department of Social Services, Division of Day Care.

Since 1965, Clarice Kestenbaum, M.D., has been the consulting psychiatrist to our program. We appreciate her sensitive supervision and her profound help in the preparation of this book.

We would like to thank Fred Pine, Ph.D., Zanvel Liff, Ph.D., David Wolitzky, Ph.D., and Sherman O. Schachter, M.D., for the use of their papers describing the Therapeutic Nursery Group program. Dr. Schachter, in addition, gave us the benefit of his comments on the early chapters of the book. Special thanks to Mrs. Elsbeth Pfeiffer, Director, Special Education of Bank Street College, for her active interest in the program, and for sharing her extensive knowledge unstintingly.

Our thanks also to Robert Taft, who reworked the first tentative efforts, and to Ms. Debora Tax, who typed the manuscript.

The program described in this book could not have proceeded without firm institutional support. In this connection we owe a special note of thanks to Mr. Dan Carpenter, director of the Hudson Guild Neighborhood House, and to the board of the Guild.

Introduction

In 1965 I first began my work as the consultant child psychiatrist to the Therapeutic Nursery Group of the Hudson Guild. During the next six years, I became increasingly impressed by the results of working with disturbed pre-school children in this unique program. These were children whose psychopathology was detected while they were still quite young so that early intervention was not only possible but instrumental in helping them overcome their difficulties. Most of the children were able to go on to first grade, an accomplishment which could scarcely have been contemplated without therapy. Part of my job as consultant was to supervise the teacher–therapists and to conduct didactic seminars for the regular nursery teachers as well. Most of the discussion at these seminars centered

around issues of normal development. In preparing my
lectures, I realized that there was a vast new literature
on the subject. I wrote this introduction, therefore, with
the teacher in mind who—having completed a program
in early education and having perused the scientific literature of psychoanalysts, behavioral psychologists, sociolo-
gists and educators—has emerged from all this thoroughly
confused. Virtually hundreds of articles have appeared in
this literature on the subject of early childhood during the
past five years. Such basic questions as "Does the mother's
talking to the baby facilitate later learning?" or "Can an
infant become 'spoiled' by too much hugging?" are subjected to scientific scrutiny—questions our grandmothers
would scoff at, let alone spend a nickel of research money
answering. Nonetheless, such research is now cloaked in
scientific respectability; the resultant answers have greatly
added to the body of information about how babies develop.

Middle class children have been attending nursery
school in this country for fifty years and the data on the
question: "Is nursery school good for you?" point to the
fact that most homes cannot provide the richness of the
nursery school environment. A child's *social* abilities will
be greatly enhanced by nursery school attendance,
although intellectual achievement (as demonstrated by a
rise in I.Q., for example) has not been increased *except*
for the child who originally came from an unstimulating
environment—"the disadvantaged child."

Philosophies in nursery school education have diverged
in the last ten years along two broad lines. The "traditional"
school contends that readiness for learning is determined
by the child's own development, and that creativity, play,
self–expression, and exploration are the primary paths
through which true learning occurs. The "cogni-

tive–developmental" school, by contrast, holds that early stimulation in such tasks as recognition of letters and numbers and classification exercises can be done formally in nursery school, and that untapped intellectual abilities were, in effect, wasted by not being used until the first grade. In fact, the conflict between the two opposing views is largely theoretical. In practice, most schools are not oriented toward either extreme but are somewhere in between. What is at last being studied by the social scientists as the most important single factor in determining whether or not a child succeeds in school is the teacher herself: her own particular style, her mode of interaction with her class.

If confusion exists in the ranks of nursery teachers who do not know whether to follow the example of a Dewey or a Montessori, what about the problems that confront those who work in day care centers and Head Start programs with the culturally deprived child? Does this child differ in fundamental ways from a middle class child on cognitive and social developmental scales; if so, what is the nature of the difference, when did the differences begin to manifest themselves, and what caused them? Head Start was founded in 1965 on the premise that many of the hard core poor or psychosocially deprived children had major cognitive and emotional deficits requiring intensive preschool intervention if they were to "make it" in the first grade. Many of the programs established for this group of children involved a highly specialized curriculum emphasizing language development and concept formation. In those instances when a home–intervention program was used in combination with the cognitive "push," the results showed that the intellectual functioning of disadvantaged children could be raised considerably and that if follow–up programs were continued beyond preschool years, the gain could be maintained. However, it soon became apparent that certain children were unable to take advantage of the enriched curriculum. In fact, these children could not maintain an interest in any activity longer than a few minutes, had little capacity for making friends, and did not seem to relate to the classroom teacher, even on a one–to–one basis. Some examples come to mind from my experience as consultant to the Hudson Guild. I was asked to see one little girl, who sat rocking in a corner, eyes downcast, thumb in mouth, unresponsive to the teacher's request to join a play–group. Another child was running in random fashion across the playground, striking anyone in his path. If I were to try to describe those features common to such children, I have to speak in negatives. They were usually not able to perform some of the age–appropriate cognitive tasks such as naming colors or numbers, but far more significant was the feature common to all—the lack of joy. Some were depressed or apathetic, but those who did play, like the boy in the playground, did so in a driven, repetitive, even stereotyped way. When they played with paints or blocks, there was little spontaneity. They had few friends, if any, and did not engage in the make–believe play children of three and four delight in, imitating their parents. In those day care centers which employ a psychiatric consultant (only 10% have them at the present time) the teacher can request a consultation, just as a middle class nursery can refer a child for a private evaluation. But if the treatment plan includes individual psychotherapy or even a special therapeutic nursery school, the expense may prove prohibitive; meantime, clinic waiting lists are long. As an alternative, special innovative programs, such as the one presented here, have clearly demonstrated the possibility of successful intervention with the preschool child. In the Hudson Guild program, the primary therapeutic experience takes place in the therapeutic playroom and the primary goal of the teacher–therapist is to lead the disturbed child back onto the path of normal development.

I have attempted to summarize briefly three different approaches to preschool education. It should be kept in mind that no matter what the philosophical orientation of the school, there are always a few children whose behavior does not conform to the required norms for that school. These children are not so atypical that they would immediately be excluded (severely retarded or psychotic, for instance), but soon they become labeled as "problems" who need special handling. In many schools help is either quickly obtained or the "problem" is asked to leave the school. The quiet problem child is often just left to his own devices until, say, his third grade teacher discovers he hasn't learned anything. The noisy ones are more visible and far more troublesome. They are the first to receive the benefits of the complete consultation, proving the old saw, "The squeaky wheel gets the grease." Recently, a number of schools have attempted to treat such children within the classroom. Although the model presented by the authors is based on experience with a day care population and includes a number of culturally deprived youngsters, I feel that the program could easily be replicated in any nursery school willing to try.

I was once asked, during a seminar on normal child development, why child psychiatrists always refer to children metaphorically as plants—either they "unfold like flowers in the sun" or fail to thrive like "stunted trees." The Garden Theory of child development is a singularly popular model.

Surprisingly enough, there are some developmental themes not based on a biological model (Learning Theory, for example). However, two of the giants in the field, Freud and Piaget, have as a common link a biological model which is based on the theory that every child passes through a series of fixed developmental stages. Each is set in motion by a maturational time clock; one stage has to be successfully completed before a more advanced level is reached.

In Piaget's cognitive theory, psychological development is self–generating. The succession of stages from primitive thought processes to complex problem–solving is innate and the process follows a predictable sequence. Psychoanalysis, in contrast, contends that the environment is highly influential in determining the successful arrival or arrested development at any given stage. Furthermore, according to this theory, the child's early intervention with this environment shapes his personality and profoundly affects his adaptation throughout life. Undoubtedly, my own theoretical approach has a bias because of my particular training as a psychoanalyst. Psychoanalysis is, of course, a theory which evolved from the reminiscences of adult patients, their free associations, and their dreams as they attempted to reconstruct their own childhood. From these early memories Freud's theory of personality development evolved. Direct observation of children did not occur until the 1940's when child analysts such as Anna Freud and Melanie Klein actually looked at children and played with them. Doll play and story-telling took the place of adult free associations, contributing greatly to the vast psychoanalytic literature.

Most people who work with young children are on safe territory when they examine children as young as two. The child can, after all, talk to us, tell us what troubles him, or at least reveal it in play—but what about a toddler, or more difficult yet, a three–month–old infant? How do we know what he perceives? There is an enormous body of recent research on the first few months of life, and the significance of earliest events are now more than ever considered to be of primary importance to future development.

In this introduction, I cannot attempt to discuss in detail the various theories of child development, but it is very important for all those working with young children to have a clear idea of "normality." In this way they will recognize pathology more readily and be in a better position to institute early treatment. I would, therefore, like to outline some of the fundamental characteristics of each developmental stage of early childhood. Hopefully, such a model will facilitate assessment of the individual child and help answer the question, "At what stage did normal development become blocked?"

Under ideal circumstances, a baby would be born with a certain set of environmental and constitutional givens: both parents are mature, young people who, having planned for the baby initially, now eagerly await its arrival. Both parents are in good health, are endowed with an optimal genetic make–up, and are ready to assume their roles as parents. These ideal parents, furthermore, have not invested the unborn child with unrealistic expectations, nor is the child meant to replace a beloved grandparent, fulfill an unrealized ambition, or repair a faltering marriage. The new baby is accepted as an individual in his own right with his own distinct personality.

It goes without saying this ideal situation is rarely even

approximated. How many babies just "arrive" without the benefit of prenatal care or proper nutrition during the first nine months, much less the climate of emotional readiness I just described? If the infant happens to be born into a lower class family, he may, in addition, have two strikes against him already. Dr. Benjamin Pasamanick has been studying the effects of malnutrition, particularly on the fetus and young child, for the past twenty–five years. Physical size is markedly affected and, in severe cases, even brain size is diminished. There is a high correlation between mental deficiency and certain prenatal conditions, notably toxemia of pregnancy, which characteristically reduce blood flow to the brain. Traumatic deliveries may do the same. There is a far greater incidence of this kind of pathology among children of the lower class. This constitutes "Strike one." If one were born with a complication of pregnancy, but raised in a middle class family, the ill effects of this condition might be overcome far more readily than they would be for a child who has the double insult of poor *intrauterine environment plus the stress of the lower class extrauterine environment*. The latter constitutes, for the child from a disadvantaged family, "Strike two."

There are many children from all strata of society who exhibit a subtle form of brain damage characterized by short attention span, irritability, and, later, learning difficulties. For such a child, early diagnosis of "minimal cerebral dysfunction" (as it is known) is extremely important; specific medication can alleviate many of the symptoms in most instances, and special restructuring of the child's school day can prevent the "emotional overlay" which otherwise may result from the child's handicap. (Many children may exhibit similar symptoms, so that only a medically trained specialist should make the diagnosis; medication should be given only when there is positive neurological evidence of the disorder.) The preschool teacher may be the first person to recognize the symptoms, as was true at the Hudson Guild on a number of occasions. Even the "ideal family" as I presented it can produce a brain–damaged child, and all the maternal warmth and understanding may not be enough to overcome the developmental block (which is already present from birth) without subsequent professional help.

In the first few months of life, the new baby typically spends a good part of his waking day close to the mother. Although it is the time in life when he is most dependent upon her for his most basic needs—nourishment and protection—we also realize that he is far from helpless. In fact, he is fully equipped at birth with a large repertoire of behavior patterns, or reflexes, all serving to bind him closely to the mothering figure. John Bowlby, a psychoanalyst greatly influenced by the ethologists, speaks of them as attachment systems upon which subsequent learned behavior is organized. For example, a full–term baby can suck vigorously; after a few feedings he has learned to control the rate of flow. He can grasp and cling, follow with his eyes, cry, and, after a short time, smile. We now recognize that the baby craves more than food or relief from pain. He needs the warmth of his mother's body—the touching, caressing, fondling, the sound of her voice, and the gazing at her face. She needs him, too, for the mother–child relationship is just that—a symbiosis involving two people in which both are enveloped in an exclusive, mutually satisfying world. Each comes to know the other's rhythms in a wordless communication which flows from one to the other. The mother becomes acutely sensitive, tuned in to the baby's needs. It is well known that a woman who can sleep through police sirens and fire engines may awaken the moment her infant whimpers.

Whether or not a baby is nursed or bottle–fed is less important to the eventual outcome of his development than the manner in which he was fed. The bottle, offered with tenderness, can certainly give satisfaction; still, most mothers who nurse speak of the intense pleasure they themselves experience while feeding their babies at the breast. To an observer, the baby looks the picture of bliss.

The infant cannot yet grasp the distinctness of his mother as a person, nor does he clearly distinguish himself from the immediate environment. Likewise, he may not "feel" any emotion akin to pleasure, but he is most certainly aware of unpleasant sensations and has ways of making his discomforts known. The mother, for example, may be feeding the baby when he suddenly frowns, kicks his feet, and cries. She has to interpret that cry and decides a gas pain has caused transient abdominal distress. A gentle pat and the crying stops. The mother learns, through trial and error, to interpret the infant's cries until such time as language replaces guesswork. A baby thus signals his mother hundreds of times a day. The crying can be viewed as an effective "instrument" in bringing about relief. If the mother is consistent in responding to the baby's cries, as well as to his numerous other cues, the baby begins to learn that what he does can set in motion a predictible and favorable change in the environment. Through thousands of such events, he learns to interpret the world in a systematic, organized manner. These events become enregistered, connected one with another, through associative links to form what we may now properly term a rudimentary memory.

The early period of infant development we have just been describing was referred to by Freud as the "oral stage," the mouth serving, in his view, as the chief bodily center of gratification.

It is a period of "getting–taking in," exploring the universe through the mouth, which Renee Spitz calls "the cradle of perception." But the term "oral," properly speaking, should include taking in through *other* sensory modalities as well; we now know that an infant's vision is far better in the first few days of life than we originally thought possible.

For example, a colleague, Dr. Stephen Bennett, demonstrated that if he places his face six inches from a newborn's and then slowly moves his head to one side, the infant's eyes will follow the moving face within a few hours after birth. The infant seems to prefer moving objects to stationary ones, complex patterns to those less complex. By eight weeks he gazes longer at a face than at any other object (*any* face if viewed from the front, even a mask). At about the fourth month the baby will begin to recognize the mother's face as *special*. It is difficult to describe the rich variety of responses, the complexity of the interaction that has been developing day by day between the mother and baby.

Much vocalizing and face–to–face gazing occurs between the mother and child in this phase of development, both phenomena serving to bind the two more closely together.

But even more important in this respect is another phenomenon of the early "oral" period: mutual smiling. All mothers report fleeting expressions they interpret as smiling within the first few weeks—what the dubious pediatrician has called "gas smiles." At six to eight weeks the infant does smile at a number of stimuli (viz., sounds, mobiles, faces), but by twelve weeks baby and mother begin to exchange smiles directly in response to one another. We regard this as the first true sign of *socialization*.

Nothing elicits warmer, more protective, loving feelings in the adult caretaker than the smile. The baby smiles; the mother smiles back (which psychologists say "reinforces" his smiling), and a circle of ever-expanding intimacy has been set in motion.

The early reciprocal play that characterizes human relatedness in the first months has been investigated extensively by David Schecter. The first game all babies delight in, peek-a-boo, is, he notes, the first mutually responsive communication with a love object. The child can evoke a social response even when he is not hungry or wet. This positively stimulating playful pattern of response is produced in relation to another human being.

At this point the social bond is fragile: Mother's face is but a fleeting image. As with the rattle now dangled in front of him, now quickly removed, images tend to be "out of sight, out of mind." It appears (associated with comfort and relief of distress) and disappears without warning; but from the second six months of life to the end of the second year, the baby learns that objects have permanence: even though Mother disappears, for example, she will, indeed, return. Some babies, at around seven months, may scan the mother's face intensely when a stranger appears. Others may scream with fright at the appearance of a new face, even in the presence of the mother. This "stranger anxiety," a prelude to "separation anxiety" of a few months hence, is a sign that the baby is learning to discriminate Mother, who is all important, from *Not–Mother*. It is only when the mother's image has been firmly internalized that we can speak of "object–constancy." Beforehand, the social bond is still tenuous and fragile. Under normal circumstances mothers sense this and intuitively exercise great care lest this bond be prematurely and hence traumatically ruptured.

I have spoken of the mothering figure as the one person who tends the baby's every need. Of course, the situation is rarely so simple, nor is it, in my opinion, necessary for the mother to be the *sole* caretaker. Fathers, siblings, nurses, etc., are all part of the developmental experience as I have outlined, but these latter are, nonetheless, perceived at the outset as alternate mothers.

A working mother, as long as she is secure in the knowledge that a responsive caretaker is available and responding to the baby's needs, can establish the desired bond in those hours she does spend with the baby each day. In this instance, the baby learns soon enough that the person who gets up at night, the one who doesn't go away on weekends, who doesn't leave though some others may come and go—that one is Mother! She smiles the most, baby notices; she kisses the most often; it is she who greets him with the most enthusiasm.

Ideally, a mother would not leave her baby for any prolonged period within the first two years; if she must, however, a familiar caretaker may allay many of the baby's fears. There is no way to remove all frustration or anxiety from the baby's life in any case. Ultimately, the baby must learn that his mother cannot always come the moment he cries. What is important is the consistency of his care overall, and the predictability of his environment.

What I have depicted here is the beginning of *attachment* in infancy, along with some of the factors central to this most essential step. This attachment step is the cornerstone of successful adaptation. The mother–child bond is the prototype for all future relationships. As such the manner in which the child is destined to relate to those around him is highly colored by the nature of this bond. In this sense a child's trust, or his suspicions, his warmth toward others, or his hostility are in large measure to be understood as outgrowths of the success—or failure—of this developmental stage. Once the importance of attachment was recognized as the crucial first step toward socialization, students of child development began to be concerned with the causes of *nonattachment*.

We readily distinguish three principle avenues to the latter condition. The first involves factors inherent in the child; next, those peculiar to the mother; finally, those relating to the evolving familial and extra–familial environment.

As I noted earlier, some children are born with certain neurological problems that prevent them from responding normally. Such babies might not, for example, follow a moving object with their eyes or interact with the mother by babbling or smiling. Mothers of such infants often feel "shut out" and thus turn away from them, experiencing none of the joyful interchange they might share with a normal infant or which they indeed already share with their other children. Here the mother's reaction—and this would be typical of the situation with autistic children—is a response to a problem inherent in the child. The mothers of such children, incidentally, need and merit a great deal of sympathy regarding the heavy burden of guilt and depression with which they invariably struggle. All too often their sense of blameworthiness would be aggravated by professionals who tended to accuse them of being the primary cause of their child's pathology.

The second source of failure to attach truly stems, however, from problems intrinsic to the mother. She may, in one common example, be suffering from a postpartum depression and be unable, as a result, to respond to her infant's frequent demands. She would, to cite another example, herself be the product of such inadequate mothering that she never properly learned how to be a mother; hence, she feels overwhelmed and totally unable to meet the hundreds of daily tasks required of her. Thus, feeding, rocking, diapering, alertness to the rapid fluctuations in her infant's "state,"—all these components of normal mothering—are experienced by her as "too much." In extreme cases we find the mother so unable to respond to her infant's cries (even though she may go through the motions of proper feeding and dressing) that the baby soon "gives up"—he literally learns "hopelessness," discovering that nothing he does effects a change for the better in his environment. Such a baby becomes apathetic, looks depressed, and gradually comes to lose the natural curiosity innate in all human beings. To go a step further, with those infants subjected to the total absence of warm mothering, such as those described by Spitz or Bowlby, the results are still more devastating. Those institutionalized children in their studies, who received only the barest minimum of relatedness and care from their surrogate mothers, eventually showed severe mental and physical retardation, even though they were normal at birth. Those who survive such intense deprivation become, for the most part, rootless, delinquent adolescents and isolated adults, who live their lives without hope or trust, totally lacking the ability to establish human bonds.

The final set of factors that may interfere with proper attachment involves the environment. These factors are extremely complex. Recently a great deal of research from this standpoint is being devoted to the "high–risk" families of the poor. Bettye Caldwell, in particular, has studied this population extensively as part of her effort to develop more effective preschool intervention programs. One illuminating fact to emerge from her investigations concerns the so–called child–to–adult ratio. Childhood development, she finds, appears to progress optimally when the child is surrounded by a small number of familiar adults, who, in turn, interact with him both often and for reasonably long periods of time ("high–frequency contact").

In the typical high–risk family, by contrast, adult figures tend to be numerous and transient. Often times the older children, furthermore, are pressed into service as caretakers of the infants, so that the latter's "routine" is lax and haphazard. It is not unusual to find a five– or six–year–old girl taking complete charge of the latest baby, just as her nine–year–old brother did for her when she was a toddler.

The quality of stimulation from the environment is also important. Ideally, the child is enclosed within a family environment that is responsive to his needs and that provides him with adequate stimulation: neither more than the child can comfortably integrate nor less than his mental and physical equipment is ready for. In such a setting social learning is greatly enhanced.

Again, in the high–risk families the norm is a combination of excessive stimulation of a kind the child cannot handle, along with impoverishment of the more appropriate stimuli. Those toys, for example, that are important as adjuncts to learning (mobiles, blocks, books) are notably absent, or nearly so. Instead the noise level from the street, the television, and the coming and going of unfamiliar people is inordinately high. In many families, incidentally, the television is used as something of a pacifier; a "good" baby is the one who will sit quietly for hours staring at the screen. A child exposed to such intense and chaotic stimuli soon learns, perforce, to shut them out; this habit of shutting out becomes so entrenched, unfortunately, that he ends up scarcely able to absorb even such information as would have been of great benefit. His whole learning apparatus, in a word, becomes seriously compromised; he is condemned to grow up handicapped. Apropos of this notion of "handicap" is the work of two prominent investigators in the field of infant perception and thinking, Jerome Kagan and his colleague, Michael Lewis. They now believe that differences ascribable to social class are already discernible by the age of one. In a series of intriguing experiments, Kagan and Lewis would show large photographs to babies from two to thirty–six months old. They would then alternate between actual photographs and schematic representations (viz., drawings). Finally, they would present to the infants purposely altered versions of either type of image (i.e., a "scrambled version," where a mouth was substituted for an eye, etc.). Even from eight weeks of age, normal infants seemed to demonstrate what these authors regard as a "discrepancy principle." This they infer from the observation that the infant will look longer at an object only *moderately* discrepant from either a totally familiar one (viz., Mother's face) or a totally novel one.

At four months, for example, a baby will look longer at a "schema" of Mother's face, but during the ensuing nine months, the same schema will provoke only briefer glances. Kagan believes this reduced "fixation time" is accompanied by the baby's acquisition of a rich set of associations to the face. A different kind of thinking seems to be developing, meantime, which he calls "association thinking."

At thirteen months, the baby is again noted to look longer at the discrepant version of the mother's face. It is as if, reminiscent of our earlier discussion of stranger–anxiety, the baby is now actively grappling with the fact that "here is a face *like* Mother's, which is yet *not* Mother!" There is, in addition, a definite correlation between the duration of the infant's looking at the face ("fixation time") and social class, middle class infants spending more time in this activity than those of lower class. Even more striking, the older the infants, the stronger this correlation becomes. At four months, for example, fixation time in a lower class infant is somewhat shorter, but Kagan did not find the difference statistically significant. One has, nevertheless, the impression that the inner (mental) representation of the face is less well developed in the lower class infant compared with his middle class age–mate.

Differences in comparative fixation time by thirteen months, however, are unequivocal. Lower class children do not show the same reaction to the discrepant stimulus as middle class children; Kagan concludes that this is an outgrowth of less face–to–face contact with the mother and less reciprocal smiling and vocalizing. There has simply been less exposure to a face than would be expected in middle class homes. The one year old from the poor home is already behind in cognitive development.

This remarkable and, as far as we can tell, causally related sequence of events—less face–to–face contact in early life, impaired attachment, thence to poorer learning capacity in later life—figures as an important factor in accounting for the failure of lower class children to fulfill their intellectual potential.

Having considered "attachment," the hallmark of this earliest "oral" stage of development, I would now like to consider some of the more fundamental aspects of the next stage.

Ironically, just as the baby's primary task during the first phase was to *attach* himself to his mother, now his chief business is to *detach* himself from her, to the extent appropriate to his physiological and emotional development.

To the Freudians, this is the "anal" stage; to the Eriksonians, the stage of "autonomy vs. self–doubt," to Mahler, the stage of "individuation." But to most mothers, it is known more simply as the "terrible two's."

Now the cuddly, smiling infant is up and running, mischievous, and "into everything" as motor skills race ahead of judgment. Most mothers find this stage considerably more trying than the one before. The toddler's wish is to "do it myself;" his mother must encourage him in this, as well as in his efforts at wider exploration of his surroundings and she must stimulate his natural curiosity, yet be able to set limits and protect him from hurting himself.

Most two year olds seem "negativistic" in the eyes of adults. "No" is their favorite word. This oppositional behavior is understood by David Levy as the child's attempt to establish himself as a person in his own right. The child is beginning to have a sense of his identity as separate and distinct from the mother, although, to be sure, his view of himself is intimately related to his mother's general impressions of him. By and large, if his mother sees him as (mostly) "good," he will see himself as (mostly) "good."

It is interesting that Freud coined the phrase "anal

period" to denote this stage. The two year old, it is true, begins to derive some sensory pleasure from the activity of the anal sphincter, but more importantly, it is here that he develops for the first time some control over a part of his own body. He also exerts control over *when* he uses this power. A struggle often ensues between mother and child over the timing of bowel functioning: the so–called "Battle–of–the–Pot." This battle, however, does not begin with toilet training; with the coercive–intrusive mother, for example, the Battle–of–the–Pot was in all likelihood preceded by the Battle–of–the–Spoon.

At two, however, the child is better equipped for battle. No matter how she may cajole or threaten, the mother cannot force him to "let go."

Mothers try to win this "battle" in either of two main ways. If one were to look at maternal control along a continuum from "democratic" to "authoritarian," one could say the *democratic* mother tends to avoid conflict by sensibly waiting until the child is emotionally quite ready to train himself. The *authoritarian* mother, on the other hand, coerces and imposes her will at every display of independence including, of course, those centering around toilet–training.

Characteristically, the child from the authoritarian home is obedient, for obvious reasons. But obedience does not necessarily spring only from fear of punishment. The fear of losing the mother's love can be equally compelling. Democratic mothers sense intuitively that children are, after all, social creatures, inclined to obey those to whom they are attached. A stern glance from an otherwise warm and loving mother may be more upsetting than a slap.

Either style of mothering is conducive to the establishment of close bonds. What is crucial is not so much the

style, but the degree of maternal *involvement*. One sometimes encounters, for example, another type of mother,
whose attitudes and mode of interaction with her child
might best be described as "laissez–faire." She is aloof
and uninvolved; her behavior fails to foster attachment,
often to an alarming degree.

Besides mastery of certain motor functions, the other
important maturational step in the two year old is the
acquisition of language as a vehicle for *communication*.
Previously, language was the "autistic" babbling of the
infant—autistic, in that babies seem to derive pleasure from
making and imitating sounds independent of what effect
this has on others. But by eight or ten months, the infant's
pleasure is enhanced greatly by his being able to repeat
the sounds mother makes. Language, in the ordinary sense
of intercommunication, stems from this interplay with the
mother.

Preverbal learning of this sort, via imitation, is essential
for language development. We observe that in families
where the child is very much spoken to, even when he
does not yet seem to understand, he will develop the capacity for language *earlier* than is the case for children deprived
of such stimulation.

Once the child begins to acquire verbal labels, learning
surges forward by leaps and bounds. Words soon become
linked together in "verbal chains;" symbol formation prog-
resses rapidly; we then witness the development of concep-
tual thought.

In the culturally deprived home, this sequence is often
disrupted. Even in the absence of a neurological handicap,
many children from such homes frequently show learning
difficulties in school and do poorly on the standard vocabulary tests. A number of children unquestionably received

adequate mothering in the first year and were able to establish warm relationships. In the realm of verbal interchange, however, their experience was relatively meagre, as with children from deprived backgrounds in general. Here we might mention the work of the psychologist, Earl Schaefer. Studying the effects of a home–tutoring program for disadvantaged children, he showed that by age three, children in the control–group did worse on verbal than on nonverbal tests. He had noted that all the children were being reared in something of a conversational vacuum. There was much less talk at the dinner table, fewer bedtime stories, etc., than in the middle class home. When the parents did speak to them, it was more often to prohibit or punish than to praise or encourage. Schaefer concluded that parents of these homes must be considered poor models for language transmission.

Most toddlers, from whatever background, will eventually acquire a modicum of language skills, at which point dependency upon the mother is significantly reduced. Before this moment, there were many gesticulations and grunts only she could interpret correctly; now the child can make his needs known to other members of the family as well. Father and siblings become increasingly important. The child will spend greater periods of time away from mother—in the yard, at the playground—though still remaining, of course, within shouting distance.

In his daily excursions to the sandbox, he is learning to be, as Winnicott put it, "alone in the presence of Mother." He may look toward her only occasionally now, yet he would be terrified were she to leave him unannounced. Separation from mother remains the strongest stimulus to anxiety for children up until the age of two–and–a–half or three. At about three the average toddler trusts that his mother will indeed return, and we can therefore begin to speak of his having acquired complete "object–constancy." This important step in the mastery of his environment is a necessary prelude to nursery school which, if for no other reason, children do not comfortably enter before they are three.

Some children just beginning nursery school will cling to their mothers for weeks. A few others will run into the room with scarcely a backward glance right from the first day. The teachers should be aware that *neither* set of children has mastered separation–anxiety. The child that doesn't look back, for example, may never have made a deep attachment to his mother in the first place, and may have no strong investment in *any* relationship.

That pathological example aside, it remains true that precipitous separations are devastating for the two year old. The clinical vignette I am about to offer amply illustrates this point.

I once was asked to see a four–year–old girl who was described to me as apathetic and withdrawn. Her teacher was a sensitive woman, who tried in a dozen ways to engage her, and felt she was just not "getting through." The little girl's mother, Mrs. S., was a depressed young woman from the Dominican Republic who sadly told me Maria didn't love her anymore; she described Maria as having been happy and outgoing as an infant. When she was two years old, Mrs. S., who was pregnant again, sent Maria to live with her own mother in Santo Domingo. She felt the grandmother would be better able to care for her during her confinement as life was very difficult in New York City, and she did not want to leave her little girl with strangers. The first few days in a strange land were hard for Maria. First she cried bitterly, then she refused to eat, but soon

she was "her old self" and became attached to the grandmother. Unfortunately, the grandmother became ill
several months later and Maria was sent to live with an
aunt in a nearby town. Again the traumatic scene of grieving
and resignation repeated itself. At three–and–a–half Maria
returned to her mother in New York, "but she didn't know
me anymore." Mrs. S. reported weeping, "She didn't cry
but nothing I could do made her happy and she just ignored
me."

Maria's reaction to the repeated separation was typical.
She behaved, as every mother will testify after a vacation,
with a "Who needs you?" attitude. It is as if she said, "I
trusted you and you abandoned me. I'll never allow myself
to get close to you—or anyone—again." It was Mrs. S.'s
own feeling of rejection and her own subsequent depression which prevented her from reaching out to Maria
despite the little girl's aloofness.

This story, because of the teacher–therapist's intervention, had a happy therapeutic outcome. Unfortunately,
many other children who experience such separations
—even with kind caretakers who have the best of inten-
tions—do not fare so well.

The last developmental stage of early childhood is the
one most familiar to the nursery school teacher, encompass-
ing what is usually called the "preschool years." Those
who have chosen this age group—three to six—to teach
are often drawn to their work out of fascination with the
child in transition from infancy to school age. These years
are remarkable for the enormous changes occurring on the
physical as well as emotional levels. Coordination and cog-
nition are improving rapidly; the child is now able to control
his bodily functions reasonably well and to take some
responsibility for his personal safety. The normal five year

old has a fair mastery of language (estimates place his vocabulary in the range of 5,000 words). His grasp of syntax, furthermore, approximates that of the adult. He possesses a sense of time and space, can form concepts, and solve simple problems.

Increasing capacity to use symbols during this stage leads to abstract thinking, albeit on a primitive level, and fantasy formation. The latter is important for the working out of solutions to problems, as well as for the release of tension.

We may now speak of the child as a truly social being. He has a developing sense of himself, of his place in the family, and at his school. He learns to play with others, to tolerate some degree of frustration, to share, to delay gratification, and to better control his aggressive impulses.

On the psychological plane, the preschool child is coming to grips with the problem of *identity*. Gender role and sex–typing are fundamental self–concepts, and become established, under favorable circumstances, rather early. Three year olds, for example, are extremely interested in their bodies. They discover their genitals, and these quickly become the object of intense curiosity, not to mention sensual pleasure, all of which help account for the usual psychoanalytic rubric for this epoch: the "phallic" stage.

A boy of three regularly invests his penis with special value; he assumes everyone has this marvelous organ that can grow big, water the flowers, and make designs in the snow. He will demonstrate his prowess to any onlooker, little girls in particular. One often hears of a little boy, upon seeing his baby sister in the tub, reassure their mother, "Her penis is very little, but don't worry; soon it will grow!" Little girls, meantime, however they may come to feel later on about their feminine attributes, have somehow to explain the absence of a penis. Learning that she has a different, special organ of her own inside her body that can make babies, does not, at this stage entirely assuage her feeling of having been short–changed. The dream of a three–year–old girl of my acquaintance will serve to illustrate this point. She awoke once from a nightmare shortly after her new baby brother was brought home, and told her mother, "I dreamt I had a pee–pee like Joey's, only it fell in the toilet and drowned." Other little girls will deny their wish to have a penis by trying to urinate standing up, like their brother.

Fear of *losing* the genital becomes the major new anxiety of the phallic stage ("castration–anxiety," in psychoanalytic parlance), much as separation–anxiety occupied the central place in the period preceding.

To return our attention to the little boy, he is becoming more assertive and independent yet remaining all the while very attached to mother. He is, in fact, jealous of any diversion of her affectionate interest away from him. His chief rival in this prototypical love–affair is, of course, the father, and no matter how kind and loving the father may be in actuality, he will naturally be perceived as bigger and more powerful, hence threatening.

People have dealt with this triangular relationship in different ways over the centuries. Oedipus, the Theban king, who unwittingly kills his father and marries his mother, pays a high price for his deeds—symbolic castration—when he blinds himself upon learning the truth.

In *Jack and the Beanstalk* we see a happier resolution. Jack kills the wicked giant, takes the giant's treasures, regaining his rightful inheritance in the process, and lives "happily ever after" with his mother. It is no wonder that this tale, answering so accurately to the unconscious fantasies of the four year old, has been a favorite for many generations.

Neither Oedipus' nor Jack's solution to the problem is very satisfactory. The psychoanalysts' interpretation of what actually does happen in real life is that the boy *identifies* with his father ("If you can't fight 'em, join 'em"). In so becoming like his father, he gives up clinging to his mother, rejecting for a time his mother's kisses and girls in general; he turns toward involvement in male-oriented activities and wants to be "like the big boys."

Many children intuitively understand this. One five–year–old boy insisted on hearing *Jack and the Beanstalk* every night for a year. One day, after the giant had once again "crashed to earth with a thud, never to be seen again," he announced, "That isn't what really happened. The giant came down the beanstalk and went home to Jack and his mother and they all lived happily ever after. He was really the daddy, wasn't he?"

The process of *identification* does not appear overnight. It is preceded by years of imitating parental behavior. The toddler puts on his father's hat and tie and tries to behave "like daddy." A little girl will act out with her dolls what she experiences at home.

Parents serve as models for their children who in turn incorporate some of their complex patterns of behavior, personal attributes, and characteristics. A loving parent is more likely to be taken for a model than a rejecting one. Conscience formation is also a product of *identification*.

At first parental *prohibition* becomes internalized. For example, a three year old might not molest a kitten for fear of getting spanked, even though his mother is not present. Later, *ideals* become internalized. A five year old might not hurt the cat because his parents would not, and he has incorporated their values. In other words, he has now an ideal self based on identification with a few key models. The child now demands from *himself* conformity to a standard of conduct. He also can identify with the cat and experiences *empathy* for it. Parental discipline based on a close affectionate relationship with the child, rather than threats of punishment, fosters the development of such feelings.

The solution to the oedipal problem is the most significant accomplishment of early life, particularly for the boy. It depends on the child's adaptive capacity, his ability to cope with overpowering *inner* drives as well as with external reality. If he can find his way unscathed through this period, he can undoubtedly handle the many minor skirmishes which he will face thereafter in his day to day life. He learns to cope with envy of a friend or sibling, loss of a beloved pet, and can defend against numerous transient fears of childhood. Poor models, of course, make the task difficult and result in maladaptive solutions. A five–year–old boy with an excessively harsh father might, for example, take for his own those same characteristics he so fears and become the school bully. Another child with such a father might identify with his mother and exhibit transvestite behavior, wearing girl's shoes and skirts.

Again, there may be no father figure to serve as a model, so often the case in broken homes. The examples of maladaptive behavior and symptoms in the neurotic preschool child are too numerous to mention and would fill a textbook of psychopathology. Each situation deserves its own diagnostic evaluation. Nevertheless, it behooves a teacher to know whether a child exhibiting infantile behavior is simply being immature or whether his behavior represents a temporary regression. Children often "return" to an earlier developmental stage as a reaction to a disturbing event, such as divorce or the birth of a sibling. Whenever the teacher has doubts about the mental health of a particular child, she should decide first of all whether the child is capable, to paraphrase Freud, of love, work, and play. If he can achieve all three, he most likely does not need therapeutic intervention.

An understanding of normal development is necessary before psychopathology can be identified and seen in its proper perspective. Even children with severe developmental problems can almost invariably be helped, once the current diagnosis has been established.

Here I would like to express my clinical optimism. Children *can* be helped; they are malleable and their patterns of behavior not yet so fixed as to resist our interventions.

Just as important as the correct diagnosis is the formulation of a treatment plan. This should be tailored specifically to meet the needs of each individual child. The teacher–therapist must be able to supply the warmth and nurturance a particular child may have been missing. She must not only be aware of his feelings, she must help him differentiate feelings or moods he may experience as blurred and ill–defined. She acts as a link to the larger world that stretches beyond home and school. She acts as translator, making the maladaptive aspects of his behavior comprehensible to parents and other teachers while the child is mastering better social skills. The teacher–therapist's task is, in a word, to get through to the child. It is not so important just what method she employs. Rather she becomes, in her very person, the instrument through which the damaged child regains himself.

Clarice Kestenbaum, M.D.

The
Emerging
Child

Chapter 1

Background and Development
of the Hudson Guild's
Therapeutic Nursery Program

THE CHELSEA district is approximately one square mile where trucks rush by. The playground is a fenced off bit of concrete, and projects loom unimaginately, repetitively, and impersonally. The cast of four and five year olds is as varied as its ethnic backgrounds and personal histories. The behavior runs the gamut from buoyant play to heated tantrums and listless inaction.

Enthusiastically drawing a family scene, Alex calls to Susie to congratulate him on his picture. Debby sings softly to a doll, while Carol sets the table for a game of house. Derek and Gary discuss the wisdom of placing yet another block on their mammoth tower structure, and Linda bubbles over to all listeners with news of her trip to the circus. Paul and Douglas take turns loading the dump truck with

3

wood, while Nancy prances about jauntily in her costume of high heels and bridal veil.

The classroom scene, however, is hardly one of unalloyed childhood gaiety. Uninvolved with toys or peers, Seth, a sallow–skinned four year old, sits hunched sadly in a corner. Three fingers fill his mouth. With apparent nonchalance, fat Carmella knocks over a complex block building, which was industriously constructed by others. Maria, wistfully eyeing groupings of children, stands in silent exclusion. Harry shrieks excitedly and unintelligibly, seizing and then quickly thrusting aside any toys belonging to his peers. Lethargically trailing behind the teacher, Sue continuously whines, no matter what gestures are made to interest or appease her. Meanwhile, Juan, in constant battle for possession, engages in conflict after conflict, using classmates as punching bags, and Chris repeatedly breaks up any group activity or incites others to do so.

It is for these latter children, who visibly manifest signs of emotional disturbance, that the Therapeutic Nursery Group (TNG), functioning within an existing day care center in the Hudson Guild Neighborhood House, was first established.

The Neighborhood House was founded in the early 1900's to meet the needs of the then predominantly Irish, Greek, and Italian population of the Chelsea district. It now services a large number of black, South American, and Puerto Rican families as well. In 1943, the Neighborhood House set up a day care center for the children of working mothers and others who needed their children attended to from 8:00 A.M. to 6:00 P.M. Careful consideration was given to the needs of young preschoolers by professionals in the field of early childhood development. The planners arranged for an appropriate ratio of children to adults, adequate indoor and outdoor space, proper rest facilities, balanced meals, nontoxic equipment, as well as play and educational materials.

Despite the founders' remarkable foresight, the teachers at the Hudson Guild's Day Care Center discovered within a short time that they had many children whose problems were extremely difficult to cope with in the normal nursery school situation. After careful study, the Hudson Guild's Mental Hygiene Clinic recognized that a different treatment approach was needed for these children. Since many of the developmental tasks of preschoolers are in the area of social adjustment, it was decided that group therapy with five children meeting twice weekly for an hour under the supervision of a teacher–therapist would produce significant results.

Thus, in 1956, the Mental Hygiene Clinic joined with the Day Care Center staff to give birth to the Therapeutic Nursery Group (TNG)—an experimental program in therapeutic nurseries. Now the therapeutic team consists of a director, a consulting child psychiatrist, a psychologist, two teacher–therapists, and the clinic's social work staff, all of whom work with the regular nursery school teachers.

The team screens the children who manifest disturbances in the regular nursery classroom to see if they might benefit from joining the TNG. Symptoms of some problem children include withdrawal (inhibition, inarticulateness, submissiveness), immaturity (overdependence, low frustration, overcompliance), temper tantrums, hyperactivity, and overaggressiveness. Difficulties common to various symptom profiles include impairment in impulse control, basic trust, independent functioning, self–identity, and reality testing. Each child has one or two key problems which are the focus of the teacher–therapist's intervention.

The TNG is a special experience designed to enhance that of the child in the larger day care center. Its aim is

progressive emotional development and socialization for
the disturbed child evaluated in terms of the child's
increased relatedness, adaptive behavior, emotional stabil-
ity, a growing ability to cope, and a decrease in such symptoms as tantrums, moodiness, depression, and whininess.
The basic rationale of this program is that the early detection and treatment of these psychological disturbances
serve as constructive influences on the child's current and
subsequent personal and social adaptation. The Therapeutic Nursery Group offers clinical evidence that such
a corrective emotional experience is an effective mode of
intervention.

In an unpublished paper, Dr. Zanvel Liff has pointed
out the underlying reasons for team work. "The outstanding
similarity of the regular day care and therapeutic nursery
is that the children in both are in a preschool educational
program with teachers who are interested in them, who
accept and respect them, and who work with them to expand
their horizons. In both, the child is helped to cope with
his first separation from his mother, to use his growth potential in his association with his peers, and to increase mastery
through play materials and activity. Teachers offer encouragement when needed and impose limitations when necessary. Along these dimensions the therapeutic nursery program and regular nursery school groups are alike.

"The differences between them must be viewed as qual-
itative gradations. The general day care class is primarily
educational in purpose; it has twenty children for forty–five
hours a week. Its therapeutic aspects are implicit, but are
not especially focused on the specific problems of the emotional growth and development of the individual child. The
TNG is set up for the purpose of meeting the therapeutic
needs of specific children, of focusing emphasis upon the

feeling responses of two groups of five children for two hours a week."

In the familylike closeness of the TNG setting, the child relates to his peers with more involvement and to his teacher–therapist in a heightened manner. The diluted relations of the large classroom are gone. With her specialized skill and knowledge of childhood problems, the teacher–therapist can increase her impact on the child's emotional growth and constructively intervene to alter his self-image. This familylike structure is extremely important in the Therapeutic Nursery Group, since the dynamic interacting forces within the group develop with a great deal of intensity. For example, there is the rivalry to exclusively possess the teacher–therapist (parent figure) and the struggle for positioning in the TNG (the family).

Central to TNG is the attempt to engage the child in a process of emotional relearning which will result in a realistic self–appraisal. With the liberating attitude of the teacher–therapist, the child with a constricted ego has an opportunity to expand his self–concept. By clarifying feelings for the child—feelings which relate to himself, to his impact on others, and to the impact of others on him—the teacher–therapist helps the child to function more independently, to accept himself, and to attain greater ego strength. Acting as a stable, consistent, supporting, nurturing figure, she reinforces all that is growth–producing in the child. She interprets material that is relatively close to awareness in a rational, sympathetic way, thereby helping the child to assimilate and understand difficult situations and to cope with them more effectively. The reality of a given piece of behavior is made clear: "Peter plays there and you play here, but Peter still likes you and will play with you again" (Lambert and Schoor, 1958). It is with her role that the child identifies by internalizing this type of growth experience, and he begins to relate to himself in a healthier way. Essentially, the teacher–therapist, through her attitude —without much talk, without much ado—frees the child's ego strengths and positive resources.

Aside from the methods used by the teacher–therapist—which will be described in detail in the case histories recorded here—the small, intensive group setting itself acts as a therapeutic agent. Here, the introverted, retiring, inconspicuous child who grows up unnoticed by family and community is given attention by his peers and elders. The destructive, impulse–ridden child learns by various kinds of group pressure those inner controls which are needed for socially acceptable behavior. Finally, the group promotes the infantile child's desire to learn, develop, and relate to his peers. The child returns from the small group's intensive atmosphere to the larger social unit of the ordinary classroom, and his teacher, who is aware of his problems, helps him to reinforce and adapt what he has learned to a wider, more realistic environment.

One can only surmise what effect this early detection and treatment has on the entire tone of the regular nursery room in relieving and supporting the nursery school teacher, who is trying to cope with many, multi–level children. Ours is not a therapeutic nursery, but a *therapeutic group within a normal nursery school.*

The therapeutic group working within a normal nursery school functions simply enough to be duplicated by almost any day care center. Since the value of such therapeutic groups for disturbed children of no private means is unquestionable, the following pages are devoted to a description of the TNG's organization and an analysis of the therapeutic methods employed. We have chosen to present the bulk of our material as case histories of some of the children involved in the TNG program. Such a procedure will clarify the dynamics of group activity and will represent the development of each individual child as it was first recorded.

Chapter 2

We Find Each Other

ALTHOUGH the Therapeutic Nursery Group functions as a team, the role of each individual staff member is clearly delineated. The TNG director is responsible for the overall integration of the program. Furthermore, she conducts one of the special therapy groups and oversees the training of another teacher–therapist who conducts the second group.

The TNG director works hand in hand with the director of the Day Care Center, whose role is complex, time–consuming, and vitally important to the TNG's functioning. Fundamental to its success is the attitude of the director of the Day Care Center, who promotes the emotional climate necessary for the acceptance and implementation of the TNG program as well as the cooperation between the therapeutic team and the regular staff. The director can facilitate a team approach by making time available for meetings and encouraging the interchange of information in casual ways. She is the principal link between the teachers and the TNG.

The child psychiatrist supervises the ongoing work of the program. She tests each child to reach beneath symptoms and unearth the dynamics of behavior. She observes the group's activities and, during these or in later discussion sessions, advises the teacher–therapists about both the behavior which has been displayed and the direction the therapy should take. When drug therapy is indicated for an individual child, she has, with her medical background, the authority to initiate it.

Each child in the program is evaluated by the psychologist. The Stanford-Binet, Bender-Gestalt, Draw a Person, CAT, and Rorschach tests are used. These, together with the psychiatrist's report, help to give an overall clinical picture of the child and delineate his learning capacities.

Since many of the problems which the TNG children suffer from are a result of environmental factors, the social workers on the team try to work directly with the families of the children involved. Some of the most difficult tasks the TNG faces lie precisely in this area of contacting families and eliciting their understanding and help for the child.

It is the teacher–therapist, however, who holds the core position in the TNG. The program is only as good as the competence of the individuals using the theoretical framework. Therefore, particular attention is paid to selecting the TNG teacher–therapists. In addition to the usual education requirements and early childhood and nursery school experience, these teacher–therapists must have a working knowledge of clinical diagnosis as well as therapeutic theory and technique. The teacher–therapists are chosen for their warmth and flexibility, their willingness to learn and grow professionally, and their ability to deal with symptoms quickly and calmly. They must also be able to impose limits and controls, for an atmosphere of total permissiveness would only hinder those children whose disturbances have been caused by repeated frustration.

Finally, the role of the regular day–care–center nursery school teacher is extremely important to the TNG. These teachers work with the TNG whenever a child from their class is involved in therapeutic treatment. Since they spend as many as forty–five hours a week with the children, they can quickly spot a child whose behavior interferes drastically with his ability to function, and they are invaluable in reinforcing treatment goals.

The nursery school teacher is a necessary adjunct to the therapeutic process because her training in early childhood education makes her aware of the significance of the children's behavior and of the meaning of play. If her experience is accompanied by an imaginative flexibility, then the teacher can devise ways of dealing with individual behavioral difficulties and coping with them in a group setting.

Close collaboration between the regular nursery school teachers and the TNG staff creates a situation in which even the most disturbed children can be reached. It further ensures an ongoing professional growth and a development of therapeutic techniques based precisely on the supportive interchange of team work. The clinic staff pools its skills, findings, and understanding of the child and makes them available for the daily program of the teacher. Thus the nursery school teacher becomes more aware of the tremendous impact of her intervention. Because of their personalities, some teachers have fewer problems relating to disturbed children and can implement the therapeutic aims more easily. A nursery school teacher who can respond differently to different children, who communicates that what the children say and do matters to her, who appreciates their efforts as much as she does the *results* of the efforts, is one who will help the children with their problems. Her sensitivity and understanding will facilitate change—whether she helps the child to develop an ability to tolerate frustration, to delay gratification, or to accept support at a time of transition.

A sensitive teacher can identify the situations that trigger behavioral conflict in the classroom. Once these keys are identified, she can then help the child understand the relationship between the situation and his behavior. In an atmosphere of respect and acceptance, the child can use this understanding to strengthen his coping devices so he may develop and grow. His grasp of reality will improve, his ability to function will grow, his sense of himself will be enhanced.

The nursery staff reaches the more difficult children through the constant exploration of alternative approaches. This experience is then shared to benefit all the children, not just those in the therapeutic program.

The TNG program is set in motion the moment the teacher–therapists begin to observe those children who have been of special concern to the teachers and the director of the Day Care Center. Perceptive observation is the primary tool for diagnosing, understanding, and planning therapy for each individual child. For a total picture of the child's behavior to emerge, frequent observations are necessary at various times during the day.

Different activities reveal different types of problems. The child's difficulties in relating to peers and adults can be pinpointed through observation. The possibilities are varied. Is his manner of relating bossy, provocative, teasing, wheedling, competitive, or belligerent? Is it antagonistic, demanding, victimizing, seductive, touchy, infantile, passive, or mischievous? Is it spontaneous, friendly, open, direct, empathetic, generous, and understanding? Finally, how appropriate is this behavior to his age group?

A child's approach to and use of materials reveals the extent to which he is using his capacities in the nursery school situation. Is his use of these materials organized, imaginative, explorative, enthusiastic, and satisfying? Or is it stereotyped, inhibited, disorganized, anxiety–provoking, or, finally, sterile and destructive?

The way a child handles the nursery school routines further clarifies his behavioral problems. During transitions does he dawdle or move easily into a new activity? Does this change provoke disorientation, wildness, apprehension, or withdrawal?

Other aspects of the child further clarify a total clinical picture. The pitch of his voice, his use of language, articulation, and vocabulary are central. Of importance, too, is the primary way in which he appears to learn and to relate: listening, hearing, feeling, or touching. How does he spend his time when left on his own? What is his characteristic level of response to the world?

Three initial reports on children admitted to the TNG program provide a description of the behavior patterns which emerge from observation.

Paul has a sweet, wan smile, sallow skin, large, sad, brown eyes, which are the most prominent feature in his thin face. He looks undernourished, is shabbily dressed, and there is a depressed, resigned quality about him. He is always on the periphery of the group. He whines, cries easily, has little frustration tolerance, or involvement in or understanding of nursery school routines. He seems to have little or no sense of himself. Only when he is engaged in open conflict with another child does his forlorn quality disappear. He is restless and, although some of this may be due to fatigue, he seems generally undirected in his play. No meaningful peer or adult relationship is visible.

Merlin is an attractive, small–boned, black girl, who generally seems to be sulky, disgruntled, and unsatisfied. She seldom smiles and is frequently weary and aloof. In the playground, she was observed angrily defending a hoop, squeezing another child's neck, rejecting a friendly over-ture, and aggressively pushing another child.

George is a sturdy, large child. His eyes are deep–set, and they have an alert expression. He is impulse–driven, hyperactive, and rarely stops long enough to experience what is happening to him or what he is doing. His level of socialization is infantile. His pushing and grabbing is a disruptive influence in any group and he constantly requires an adult at his side. His voice is loud and his language demanding: "Shut up." "Go away, you fucker." "Give me that." "Don't look at me." If an adult is assisting him, he can stay at an activity until its completion; other-wise, his attention wanders. His contact with teachers seems provocative, yet there is no meaningful relationship which gratifies him. His coordination seems normal, although he does drag his feet and is occasionally seen walking on his toes.

One day, he was observed in a disgruntled, antagonistic mood. His fingers were in his mouth and nose; his posture was limp and his speech unintelligible. He was crying, whining, pushing, and shoving. He seemed totally uncom-fortable with himself. When an adult entered the room, he interrupted a circle game to run toward him, but the contact with the adult neither sustained or gratified him.

After the initial work of observation in the regular nurs-cry classroom, a screening conference is held to select children for the Therapeutic Nursery Group. The medical director of the clinic, the clinic administrator, the psychiatrist who examined the child, the social worker who interviewed the parent and received permission for the diagnostic work–up, the TNG teacher–therapists who observed the child, the director of the Day Care Center, and the child's regular nursery teacher all meet together.

If observation provides the key to unfolding behavioral patterns, then skill, knowledge, and sensitivity are needed to help a child move toward more socially acceptable and self–satisfying behavior. It is the director of the Day Care Center who initially approaches the parent, offering the testing and therapeutic services of the small group. Part of the TNG's uniqueness is that *we* approach the family, rather than wait for them to ask for help. Problems are detected in the TNG long before the usual procedure of the elementary school guidance counselor confronting parents with a disturbed child. Since the director of the Day Care Center has almost daily contact with the family when they bring and pick up the child, pay fees, discuss medical or other problems that arise during the school year, it is she who presents the child's problems to the parent in a nonthreatening way by gearing her explanation to the parent's level of understanding. She explains that the special TNG program will help the child do better in nursery school, allow him to have a happier time, and function more effectively in elementary school.

One of the frustrating aspects of the screening process has been parents' refusal to allow their child to be included in the TNG or in any other form of treatment. Sometimes the skill of the social worker can change the parents' attitude toward accepting help. At other times, nothing can be done. Some parents may consent to their children's participation

in the TNG, but refuse any counseling or therapeutic work
for themselves. When this happens—even though it is preferable for one or both parents to be involved in an ongoing
relationship with a member of the social work staff—the
child is still retained as part of the TNG. We have found
that the child's gains in the TNG result in his greater
acceptance at home. This, in turn, engenders a changed
parental attitude toward him. For example, when a child
no longer responds to each parental request with a temper
tantrum, the parents feel more adequate, can relate more
to the child's strengths, and can enjoy parenthood more.
Our experience shows that the group can help the child's
growth and development aside from, or even in spite of,
specific conflicts in the home. The child's natural push
toward healthy growth is strengthened by the teacher
–therapist's individual attention and by a close relationship with his peers in a small group.

At the initial screening conference, a tentative, dynamic
formulation of a specific treatment plan for both the parent
and the child is developed. The screening process is
twofold. It selects children appropriate for the group and
detects children with a variety of problems which cannot
be coped with within the limits of the group's activities.
Symbiotic children and children who show signs of brain
damage, retardation, or schizophrenia are not accepted for
the TNG, but are offered an alternative plan of treatment
by the Counseling Service. When indicated, referrals have
been made to Bellevue Hospital's Mental Hygiene Clinic
or to Columbia–Presbyterian Hospital's Psychiatric Institute for complete neurological and medical workups.

The selection of children to form a group, rather than
a mere conglomeration of five separate individuals, is vital.
The one year a research project necessitated the random
selection of children, the group never developed cohesive-

ness. Hence, interaction was fragmentary and controls were extraordinarily difficult to maintain. In screening for a group, age is a primary consideration. One group of four year olds and another of five year olds is formed, usually with two girls and three boys in each group. We try to have a balance of passive and aggressive children. Successful formation of a group depends largely on the common denominator of a quality called "social hunger." There are some children whose acting out is so intense that they would fragment the group and would not be appropriate.

After the composition of the TNG groups is determined, the teacher–therapists frequently visit the Day Care Center classes and introduce the idea of the TNG by telling the selected children that they will meet twice a week for a special play period. The regular nursery school teachers also prepare the children for the TNG by answering any questions they might have. Since the children have usually made some adaptation to separation from their mothers in the morning, they generally do not have any difficulty leaving the Day Care Center class with the teacher–therapist to attend the TNG. In fact, after a few sessions of the TNG, the children look forward to it eagerly as a special event.

The teacher–therapist structures the initial session with a simple statement: "We're going to meet here all together twice a week for an hour and play." No intellectual explanation is offered, such as, "I'm here to help you with your problems," or "You can talk about the things that make you unhappy." Such statements are unnecessary and beyond the comprehension of some four year olds. The initial structuring is designed to promote freedom and spontaneity.

Chapter 3

A Place to Work—

A Place to Play

THE CLIMATE of the TNG playroom is geared to establishing feelings of privacy and security. Since many of the children involved suffer from poor family relationships and deficient or interrupted mothering, it is important that this room serve as a place where they can develop an uninterrupted, trusting relationship with one adult, the teacher–therapist, and learn that a ventilation of feelings is accepted. We want the children to feel that the playroom is theirs, and some of the more articulate ones have expressed precisely this. "No one looks at you here." "It's peace; a special place."

The playroom is located just down the corridor from the regular nursery classroom. Once the group is in session, no one is permitted to enter the playroom, so that privacy remains undisturbed. The room, a large one, has been divided into sections by cabinets. This creates several intimate and secure areas where structured boundaries are clearly marked. Play materials have been carefully selected according to a therapeutic rationale. Toys should not be overstimulating or overwhelming (e.g., mechanized, battery–run cars or planes). Materials are used only to create a familiar and comfortable atmosphere for the child so that the relationship with teacher–therapist can be established and the child can gain security and build ego strength.

Chosen with the developmental and age levels of the children in mind, these play materials are often similar to those in the regular nursery group. This familiarity with the playthings at hand helps the children to feel comfortable in the special room. The toys and objects used are versatile, can stimulate intellectual growth, and can be manipulated by small children satisfactorily. Some offer opportunities for ventilating hostility and aggression. Others encourage imaginative play and permit fantasies, fears, and conflicts to be elucidated.

The Doll Corner

The doll corner is a protected, cozy spot. Dolls, white and black, large and small, lie on a child–size bed available for any kind of play. The dolls have flexible arms and legs, eyes that open and shut, and a mouth for a nipple. A bed, blankets, baby bottles, and dress–up clothes as well as these dolls help the children reveal themselves by enacting a world they know. Here, the child who is torn between remaining a baby and growing up has an opportunity to work through his problems. Here, free from the pressure of conforming to normal age expectation, he can play baby.

He has the security and reassurance that it's only make-believe. At the same time, he receives the needed satisfaction from play.

The role of the teacher–therapist is to maintain those boundaries which separate play from complete or prolonged regression. Permitting this type of regression to an infantile role can be overwhelming for the child and would be inappropriate in the TNG setting. Thus, the child is allowed to have water in the baby bottle when he is playing in the doll corner. At juice time, however, he is expected to drink from a cup like other children of his age. The intimate setting of the TNG permits the child to work through this highly personal experience without shame or derision.

The teacher–therapist also helps the child to differentiate reality from fantasy. In the secure atmosphere of the doll corner, he can repeatedly enact his night fears. He can climb into bed, cover his head, and, in an authentically frightened manner, cry, "The monster is here." Such verbalization marks the first step in learning how to cope with his fear. In the growing relationship of trust between himself and the teacher–therapist, he can develop the resources within himself to master tension–producing fears which are often the result of feeling helpless. Occasionally another child can help the teacher–therapist by taking on the role of the sympathetic, protecting adult.

The Doctor Kit

The doctor kit—with real stethoscope and play injection needles—permits the children to dramatize, and hence play out, their anxieties about medical intervention and their fears of injury or insufficient strength. If the child is about to be hospitalized, we use doll and puppet play to minimize his anxiety by familiarizing him with the procedures he will experience. It is important here to be aware of the child's feelings. A matter–of–fact response to the pain of an injection may often put the experience in its proper perspective. "It does hurt, but only for a minute," is a realistic appreciation of the child's feelings. But for some children, this may not be enough. Their fear of the doctor may be intense and stem from a deep–rooted concern with disease or bodily injury. The intensity and frequency with which they focus on such a theme provides evidence for determining the severity of the problem. Reassurance about getting better, staying whole, mirror–play, and reaffirmation of strength whenever appropriate ("You did that with your boy strength" or "You couldn't manage that last year and now you can") all help to build an image of a self –managing child. A roll of gauze used by the children to enact a variation of hurts further gives the teacher–therapist clues as to how they feel about and handle injuries. With the aid of the doctor kit, one can communicate verbally or physically: "It is scary when you hurt yourself, but one does get better. The doctor helps, teachers help."

For some children, doctor–play becomes over–exciting and sexually stimulating. Transfering this play to the dolls clarifies misconceptions, distortions, and anxiety. At times, we have stopped the doctor–play completely, saying: "This game is very interesting, but it makes you both too excited. Let's find something else to play."

The Water Table

The water table is near the doll corner. The doll bottles,

nursing bottles, sponges, soap, and bottle brushes are next to a large plastic basin filled with water. On shelves in back of the table are other kitchen utensils: a coffee pot, pots, pans, dishes, egg beater, etc. These allow the child to use materials from the most primitive level of spilling and pouring to the more advanced levels of representative home–play. The various–sized funnels, hoses, strainers, and shower heads for experimentation encourage conceptualization of science concepts. Boats of wood, rubber, and plastic are also available.

Water is a basic play material. It is one of the few materials which make no demands upon the child, allowing him acceptable, comfortable, and pleasurable sensations. There are children who are reluctant to become involved in water play and require special support to be free enough to enjoy it. Constricted children enjoy the tactile sensations of temperature change, of soap bubbles, and of soap. Scattered, disorganized youngsters have become involved for longer periods of time than they usually spend on any one other activity. They gain a sense of control and mastery when pouring water—fast or slow, a lot or a little—or while fishing with play poles with magnetic ends.

Water is a material that the child can easily manipulate regardless of his intellectual ability or physical dexterity. The level of water play changes dramatically with the level of the group. Infantile pouring may be a relaxed bridge to a relationship; coloring water with paints may be a cohesive science lesson. Hartley, Frank, and Goldensohn's *Understanding Children's Play* (1952) provides an excellent source for further description of play patterns and the utilization of nursery school equipment. Babies can be washed in the large basin. When they wash the dolls' hair, the children sometimes convey their attitudes toward having their own hair washed, as well as a great deal about their self–image and feelings about their hair.

The Block Corner

The block corner is housed in two sturdy shelf cabinets. The varied–sized and –shaped blocks become towering buildings, winding roads, railroad tracks, garages, stores, etc. The structures are often knocked down—sometimes with glee, sometimes with fear. The nearby cars and trucks zoom out of control on highways. The use of such props as the policeman, the fireman, stop signs, and traffic lights not only aid in the play, but enable the teacher–therapist to bring order to this kind of chaotic activity. The child who has difficulty in sharing a toy can more easily share a road. The overwhelmed child who sees the world as a fearful, dangerous place can spend a whole year building and destroying, and, with the aid of the teacher–therapist, always reconstructing as well. The reconstructing diminishes their sense of helplessness. For the child who seems to have no sense of space (who is always bumping into things), the blocks offer concrete learning experiences dealing with spatial relationships. The stereotyped, constricted, and inhibited child can be sparked into expanding and enlarging his concept of himself and his world. The isolated child may demonstrate a rigid, intense preoccupation with structure, detail, and balance. The block play represents the child's feeling about his experiences. In the jail, he locks up family figures or creates a room just for himself. Mommy and the new baby are closed up in a building; some houses have no people; and some are happy houses with busy families. As the children change, their block play indicates the changes.

Blocks allow the child to create any kind of structure he chooses. They allow for tangible evidence of creative thought. They also enable a child to utilize ideas and to develop geometric concepts (such as a sense of weight, size, and balance), as well as spatial concepts (over, under, through, below, above, etc.). The sense of mastery, of putting ideas into concrete form, and of emotional satisfaction in achieving, are all intrinsic values of block play. The teacher–therapist can ignite and stimulate imagination, bridging the concrete to the abstract through accessories. Color cubes can be lights, windows, or Christmas trees. String can be used as a lift, a harness, or a telephone wire. A pulley can be placed in a tall building. A ramp suggests many uses: on an elementary level it becomes a delivery chute or a sliding pond, or it can be used with cars and people. On a higher level, it can be used to illustrate a science lesson involving gravity. The arches can be designs as well as entrances for cars and animals.

The block corner, like the other areas, helps the child develop the expectation that he can complete a task. But it is the teacher in the regular nursery school or the teacher–therapist in the TNG who can constructively develop the facets of block play by consciously keeping in mind the goals and needs of the specific children. She must be sensitive and aware of her timing, know when to step in, when not to be intrusive, when to add content or verbal support. Praise should be used judiciously so that the child is responding to his own satisfaction and not the adult's. The teacher–therapist's interest, enthusiasm, and skill in helping the child become conscious of the significance of his own ideas has a great impact on him. This impact can enable him to expand emotionally and intellectually. His ideas, transferred immediately into a concrete building, enable him to experience the "I" in himself.

The Punching Bag

Certain materials, such as the punching bag, allow socially acceptable, assertive, aggressive behavior and provide relief from tension. The punching bag, chosen after much searching, is a large, inflatable, plastic Joe Palooka, Superman, or Popeye. A familiar clown punching bag was eliminated because he was a pleasant symbol for many of the children and hitting him seemed contradictory.

The child can be directed toward the punching bag rather than toward "socking" another child or the teacher. The punching bag allows the child to feel that his anger is accepted and understood. It has been used to demonstrate physical strength. "I am strong," "I'm big," "I can lift him," "I can throw him." Some of these comments express bravado, but they ultimately become reality. The inhibited child spars with the punching bag tentatively for many sessions, until he is able to punch it, curse it, and ventilate many of his feelings. The punching bag has been the tool through which some children have eventually been able to verbalize their previously inarticulate rage.

Clay

Many aspects of working with clay are similar to the punching bag in relation to tension release. The plasticine can be pounded with a mallet as long and as hard as the child desires. The clay, being malleable, can be used imaginatively to make varied objects. It can help stabilize a child who first uses it destructively and then finds he can remake what he has destroyed, if he wishes.

The Dart Board

In the entry hall there is a dart board nailed to the door. The board has simple numbers (3, 5, and 10); the feathered darts have rubber suction cups. They are always accessible to the children. We have observed that a child who is motor–driven will, of his own accord, go to the darts and work off some of his inner steam. There are four darts, so that throwing them often becomes a shared activity. At such times, the sharing has helped resolve competitiveness.

Darts can be played alone and can be a child's first experience in gratifying play, where he successfully uses visual motor coordination and achieves immediate success by hitting the target he aims at. There are children who have spent months ineffectually, passively tossing a dart. Only as they grew more assertive did they attempt to become proficient and master the skill. The teacher–therapist must maintain the structure of the game, since it can easily become too exciting and deteriorate into wild, random throwing.

Balls

Ball playing, again, uses some of the same aspects of mastery, tension release, peer involvement, and competitiveness that the darts do. The ball, however, can be used much more passively than the darts, which can spark a withdrawn, nonsocial child into play with another child. A ball can be rolled quietly and easily to the child by an adult, who gradually encourages the participation of any child standing nearby. The adult withdraws and the

children continue together in related play. Rolling a ball
supplies the child with a missing, early mother–child play
experience. This kind of experience can be nurturing for
a child who needs it.

Books

Books are usually regarded as entertainment or as teaching tools. We select books primarily for their emotional
value since the children's reactions to the books offer
insight into their feelings and attitudes. The impact of the
story is easily discernable in the group setting as the children talk about the characters and the events. They express
fantasies and feelings triggered by the story.

Maria is a book about a shy child who refuses to speak.
After numerous attempts by the neighborhood people to
encourage her, she finally talks. Her plight concerns the
other children and the resolution delights them because
many of them also have a problem communicating. This
problem may be rooted in emotional inhibition, in language
difference, or in coping with the problem of just being
heard and noticed in a large family.

Sam is a sensitive, touching story of a black child, and
takes place in his home. He approaches each member of
his family, asking them to play with him, but everyone
sends him on his way. He is sad and lonely until his unhappiness is noticed and responded to. Each child has had
this experience and relates to it.

Curious George is a book which represents separation
and reunion. It tells of mischievous doings and some of
the consequences. This book helps children bring up their
concepts of good and bad, and naughty behavior, and what
mothers and fathers do when children misbehave.

A House for Everyone, a descriptive and concrete book, has helped children relate some of their experiences at home while eating, dressing, taking a bath, going to sleep, etc. One child who did not respond to the mini–dolls, the puppets, or the other stories used this matter–of–fact presentation of routine living to pour out his struggle in coping with bedtime and dressing.

Who Lives Here is a simple book frequently requested by one group of children. The children knew the book by heart, and each one wanted a turn "reading it to the group." The enormous satisfaction of being able to interest and reach a group of peers had a wonderfully gratifying effect upon each child. Children enjoy hearing a story retold countless times. The TNG groups demonstrate this capacity for repetition when the story has special meaning for them.

Stories culled from the children's actual experiences are often very useful. The child can tell dramatically about a frustrating or frightening experience, like the child who told of watching and waiting at a window for a mother delayed much beyond closing time of the Day Care Center. By retelling the story, the teacher–therapist often helps a child assimilate and understand the event better. The child's participation in the telling aids not only in the awareness of his own feeling but also in the development of his language skills.

To develop the listening skill, one must be constantly aware of the children's reactions to the story. The teacher–therapist allows them to fill in a repetitive line, or stops to make the story personal, redirecting the child whose attention may wander. Today one can find children's books which touch on every aspect of their lives and clarify the world in which they live. In our experience, each TNG group has responded to different books, depending on its stage of development and its problems.

The Mini–World

The mini–people are family constellations. Their mini–world consists of four open, painted, shallow boxes with mini–furniture (living room, bedroom, kitchen, and bathroom). A basket filled with clothing sits near the rooms and the children can dress and undress the dolls. Open boxes are preferable to doll houses, since they permit freer–flowing, mutual play between the children, and the content is more easily observed.

Individual children use the mini–dolls to act out their home experiences and their feelings about them. Moving is a constantly repeated theme. Bathroom and bedtime are often the focus of the play. Somtimes, grandma dies. Both the realities of a harsh life and their wishes for a more gratifying family life can be acknowledged.

The mini–boxes are used to help the teacher–therapist understand the problems with which the children are trying to cope. When a child repeatedly enacts a frightening or disturbing event, we try to clarify what happened and offer empathy for the child and understanding for the event.

Chapter 4

Case Histories—
Atypical Behavior

THE ACTUAL PROCESS in the TNG play room is depicted in the interreactions, moods, feelings, exchanges, and responses in the sessions. The cases selected demonstrate the range of problems: Harry is an example of the hyperactive, motor–driven child whose behavior is not organically based; Carmella is the emotionally deprived, infantile child; Rhoda and Sue are withdrawn, constricted, depressed children; Seth is the negative, oppositional child; and Duane, Juan, and Terry are angry, volatile, aggressive children.

These cases illustrate both the dramatic changes in the children as well as the limitations of the program. The responses of the teacher–therapist to the children attempt to convey an attitude rather than that there is one "correct" response.

Primitive, Motor–driven, Self–destructive

Harry

Harry was referred to the Therapeutic Nursery Group because "he drooled, dropped things, bit, hit, and scratched." He dragged himself about and didn't seem to know where he was headed.

A tall, slow–moving, unattractively dressed four year old, his movements were purposeless. His muscle coordination was poor. He had an awkward, bow–legged gait, and, instead of grasping materials, he clutched them. His expression was remote, and his pale, grayish–white skin, flabby body, and constant drooling initially repelled the observer. He was not a child who evoked tenderness or the desire to hold or cuddle.

Accepting that some children are unattractive and difficult may present a dilemma to the teacher, whose self –image rejects such an attitude. One often hears student teachers and some teachers say that they teach because they love children (Biber and Snyder, 1948). But the problem children are not easy to love or even to like. They are often disruptive and frustrating, and do not easily evoke relationships. It helps the teacher to work in an atmosphere conducive to free discussion and to try to pinpoint exactly which aspect of a child's personality is particularly grating.

Harry's voice had a flat, toneless quality. His speech was repetitious and difficult to understand. He never spoke in complete sentences, slurred words together, and confused nouns. Hungarian was spoken at home, and the language barrier might account for his paucity of communicative skills and his hitting and grabbing to satisfy his needs.

He had no awareness of his impact upon other children. Although he sought contact with them, he treated them roughly, knocking them down to get what he wanted. Highly stimulated by contact with other children, he was in perpetual motion; yet he was never observed in any continuous play with another child.

There was a quality of longing in his response to the teacher–therapist; he stayed close to her, watched her movements, and brightened when she entered the room.

These emotional and relational difficulties, linked with what appeared to be a normal intelligence, made Harry a suitable candidate for the TNG program. Although his lack of focus made him seem unable to comprehend a situation, he was actually able to follow instructions. He was the one child in a group to perceive how to make a flower illustrated by his teacher. Furthermore, he gave evidence of a pert sense of humor. At one point, after talking with the examiner, he said: "My name is 'Little Mouse.' I write," and proceeded laboriously to write the letter H.

Fear, as psychiatric examination indicated, was his predominant emotion. His inner life appeared to be a compelling nightmare of fires, dying, being crushed, and being devoured by monsters. He felt anxious and unsafe when alone, always needing an adult to help him. His body image was poor. Except for clumsiness, no motility disorder was found. He could hop, run, skip, and jump; he was right –handed and right–sighted. The total psychiatric impression was an environmentally induced, developmental lag with severe anxiety and the possibility of childhood psychosis.

The psychologist's report noted "a loss of distinction between fantasy and reality." The report indicated average functioning when visual clues were available, but an I.Q. of only 88, with the feeling of a much greater potential. His intelligence seemed obviously normal when he did not have to depend on language cues.

Harry's mother, a woman in her forties, spoke Hungarian and understood no English. Initial permission to test Harry and enter him in TNG was obtained through an interpreter. His father had died at the age of seventy, when Harry was three years old. The social worker who did the intake interview found Harry's mother to be a sad, lonely, and terribly overburdened woman. She watched her child's every movement and had difficulty controlling him, but denied the existence of any problem. She considered herself a self–sacrificing mother and was proud of never having left him since he was born. Through the interpreter she described an easy, uneventful pregnancy and delivery. Harry was nine pounds and nineteen inches at birth. He walked well by sixteen months and spoke in sentences (Hungarian) at two years. He was not permitted to play with other children until he began coming to the Day Care Center at age three. The social worker felt that the mother was unreachable.

The mother was eventually seen by a more resourceful and talented social worker who managed to establish contact with this isolated woman, using an interpreter for the first few months and then seeing her alone when she could understand more English. The team approach and the flexibility of the second social worker were crucial to the gains made by this particular child.

At the time of his referral to the Therapeutic Nursery Group, Harry's use of material was primitive and infantile;

his paintings were mere blobs of color. His world was indeed a frightening and dangerous place.

The focus of Harry's treatment was the establishment of a warm, safe relationship in which he could ventilate fears and develop inner controls. We hoped that the negative reactions of the group to his indiscriminate grabbing of toys, as well as their acceptance of any positive ideas he might demonstrate, would enable the teacher–therapist to help him realize his impact upon others. The small group offered an opportunity to foster wholesome peer relationships.

Harry came easily to the first session in the playroom. His desperation and obvious joy in being chosen to go to the playroom resulted in a close bond between him and his teacher–therapist.

The first few sessions are exploratory for most of the children. They are subdued by the new situation, watching, waiting, and sizing up this new adult and room. The teacher–therapist sets the emotional climate of acceptance and security, laying the groundwork for a trusting relationship.

Harry spent most of the first few sessions putting people in jail, scrambling up the mini–furniture and dolls, and splashing with water, never staying with any activity he started. His conversation rambled. He was easily overstimulated, and was almost flooded by excitement, joy, or anger. His interactions with the other children were sporadic, disruptive, and incongruous with their more appropriate dramatic play.

Harry's frantic behavior necessitated his being seen alone. He was one of the few children who posed a problem as to whether or not he should be kept in the group. With individual attention, the carry–over made his continuing in the group possible. He was seen alone for ten minutes preceding each session in order to help him establish a closer bond with his teacher–therapist. Control, structure, and an attempt to develop and link up memories were now the focus of this brief time together as well as in the group sessions.

The treatment plan began the instant his teacher–therapist opened the door to his nursery room. In his delight Harry would greet her with overwhelming excitement—jumping up and down. She immediately attempted to respond to his excitement: "Harry, I'm glad to see you, too. You get excited when you see me. I can tell because you're smiling, laughing, and jumping up and down. I'll count while you jump up and down next to me as we go to the playroom."

This technique of responding to the overexcited child's mode of expressing his feelings, rather than telling him to stop running or jumping, helps him organize his inner excitement. It also helps to develop cognitive time, place, and space concepts. By recognizing his inability to stop and by using the pleasure he feels in bodily movements and rhythms, one can more easily establish a working alliance with a child. It is the springboard for his developing a feeling of being understood which develops the trust in the relationship.

In spite of the attempt to tune him in and calm him somewhat, Harry often darted out of the room, ran down the hall, and barged into the playroom, bumping into the chair in which he was going to sit. As he sat, the teacher–therapist helped Harry to relate through eye contact, use of voice, and motion. This slowed him down so that he could listen as well as be heard.

In the few minutes preceding each session, the teacher–therapist helped Harry plan what he was going to play with and recall what he had done the last time in the room. The preparation for the group session and the clear definition of what was expected of him was geared to control the flooding he experienced.

The essence of establishing contact was listening to him, picking up what he was saying, and cautiously giving it back to him, clarified in a cohesive form so he could grasp and handle it.

Harry: Da monsta comin, dey die, da fire engine, da plees, da fada die.
Teacher–Therapist: You're telling me so many things about a monster, a fire engine, the police, and a father. So many things.
Harry: Da fada die, da fada die.
Teacher–Therapist: That's hard for a boy to understand.

These were repetitive themes, which he played out via the fire engine, mini–toys, and the puppets, in both his individual and group sessions. As the team began to understand more of Harry's background, the teacher–therapist was able to reassure him that his mother was still there to take care of him. She lessened the confusion caused by his father's death by placing the event in its proper time sequence: "That was a long time ago."

The ability to communicate his bewilderment and sense of loss at the time of his father's death lessened Harry's hyperactivity and allowed his social hunger to emerge. The presessions were only necessary for three weeks, because his frantic quality and disruptiveness diminished. Now the task in his group session was to enable him to gain control of his impulses, to establish boundaries, and to become aware of his impact upon other children.

In these sessions his play was given form: monsters

were placed in jail, roads were built for the zooming cars, and a firehouse was found for the noisy, frightening engine. The aim was to help Harry untangle the confused jumble of his thinking, and he was praised for his ability to focus on single events and activities. For example, Harry was distracted and flitting from one object to another.

Harry: Da truck ... Jeffrey god it ... dat book (pulling the book away from Rhoda), I need it.
Teacher–Therapist: Harry, you want so many things—the cowboys, the hammer, the truck, the water, the book—so many things. Let's find one thing you can have fun with.

Harry approached the water table then darted to the closet. Although it looked like meaningless motion, he had remembered a doll he had seen and he grabbed it from the closet, throwing it into the large water basin. He began spontaneously to fling water all over the doll. It was difficult to get him to slow down or to bathe the doll functionally. The teacher–therapist acknowledged his enjoyment of the water play, his rhythm, and his need for a more infantile level. As Harry became more relaxed, his water play provided an opportunity to help him build control. "You can pour fast, slow, a little, a lot." In a few sessions, his potential for higher functioning was evident, as he skillfully designed a stack of five funnels of different sizes and poured water through in one continuous stream. He had a great feeling of accomplishment, repeating the teacher–therapist's words, "You're doing a good job," to himself with obvious enthusiasm.

Harry's verbal ability at this time was negligible; words did not describe his feelings, but were supplied by the adult to give understanding and form to his actions and to encourage verbalization. He needed the adult to anchor him.

On one occasion when he was picked up for the session, Harry was whining and crying; his face was badly scratched, and he was obviously very upset. In the playroom, Harry's distress became more evident as he tossed animals about and threw the teddy bear away, saying "Da mommy did it; da mommy in da movie did it."

Teacher–Therapist: Did it, Harry? Did what?
Harry: I can't tell. I can't tell in English!
Teacher–Therapist: It's hard to talk about, but it made you cry and throw everything around.
Harry: Make a mommy monster. (He then scribbled on the drawing and threw it in the wastepaper basket.)

After this Harry was calm enough to relate that his mother had scratched him when he was jumping in the movies.

This was one of the many times Harry was helped to communicate his feelings and distress to a sympathetic, supportive adult. After he related the source of his anxiety, his diffuse rage would lessen, leaving him much calmer.

As his ability to focus improved slowly but steadily, and he became aware of his developing mastery of materials, Harry experienced real satisfaction. For example, one day after flitting from material to material, he was steered to the darts, since his need for physical release was apparent. Not only did he play for fifteen minutes, but his satisfaction was touchingly displayed as he set up a little toy man to watch and cheer his good shots. "Good shot—you're terrific," he said for the little man.

At first Harry was oblivious of the other children; when

he wanted something, he grabbed it. He was constantly reminded to ask for what he wanted and reassured that he could have what he needed. The teacher–therapist tried to clarify his behavior to him. "Did you ask for it?" "Was it okay to take that?" At different times the teacher–therapist supported the passive, dependent child in the group with one of the following responses, as Harry listened: "Does Harry know you still want that toy?" "Is it all right with you if Harry takes it? Tell him and then Harry will know how you feel. Harry likes the children to feel friendly to him."

By session thirty–two, the session notes described a situation in which Harry tried to get a toy away from another child. The child refused to share and sat playing with it for some time, just to keep Harry from having it. Harry kept asking, "Finished now, Sue? My turn?" When Sue finally relinquished the toy, the teacher–therapist praised Harry for the hard, long wait and reassured him that now he could have a turn as long as he wanted.

Toward the end of the year, the notes for another session reported a fight between Harry and Seth over some fish that Harry had molded from clay. The teacher–therapist explained to Seth that Harry had made these fish and did not want to share them now. Seth could make his own. This was the first time Harry was on the other side—being grabbed from and being protected. The teacher–therapist underlined this change for him: "Do you remember when you always grabbed?" Such reminders, which acknowledge emotional or physical growth, provide positive reinforcement for the child.

For Harry, as well as the other children in the group, sharing toys or waiting a turn was a crucial area in learning to function and relate in a group. Harry suffered from a complete lack of impulse control; another child, from extreme competitiveness. Both problems precipitated similar behavior—severe temper tantrums and a complete inability to cope with sharing.

Very gradually throughout the TNG year, Harry made improvements in his peer relations and learned how to play with more spontaneity and creativity. Harry and Jeffrey set up parallel buses, using the chairs. Jeffrey got the change –maker first. Harry looked as if he were going to fall apart, but grabbed the cash register and yelled for everyone to "get on the bus." The teacher–therapist reinforced, "What a good idea. Now the game can go on." By pointing out what things are acceptable or unacceptable in a group setting, by reinforcing appropriate behavior, and patiently verbalizing each set of actions so that their effects are clear in the child's mind, the teacher–therapist helped Harry to gain a sense of inner control. When he left TNG, his drawings were up to age level and well put together. He could devise ways of coping with situations and he responded easily to verbal control.

Most significantly, his inner world, replete with fear and monsters, had vanished in the secure atmosphere of the playroom. During a class discussion, Harry revealed that he had found a healthier way of dealing with these monsters: "When I grow up, I be a policeman and go in the house and get the dead man and take him to the hospital."

Harry went on to first grade in September. Although the teacher–therapist felt further treatment was necessary to maintain his gains, he could at this time function in a classroom. He was retested after a year and the psychologist reported that his I.Q. showed an increase of fourteen points (from 88 to 102). His first grade teacher stated that he was beginning to realize his potential.

Deprived, Infantile

Carmella

Carmella instantly irritated anyone with whom she came in contact. At five she was a clumsy, grossly overweight, dark–skinned, Spanish child. Her appearance was not helped by her protruding stomach and her clothes, so tight that she usually popped out of them. Her facial expression was tense and she grimaced rather than smiled. Her movements were heavy and laborious. She was the only child in her nursery group unable to grasp a crayon or a pencil. Carmella was boisterous and she usually shrieked. "Whaaa dis . . . whaa dat?" was a constant, irritating demand for attention rather than speech intended for communication; she never showed interest in the reply. Her demand for attention always kept her within a teacher's view or hearing. She never played alone and rarely initiated any independent play or ideas, skillfully manipulating children and adults into doing things for her.

With other children she vied for position and possession, and her sustained play was limited. She always took the role of the baby, the kitten, the puppy—passively lying on her back to be fed, presenting a ludicrous picture. No play or action really satisfied her. Carmella seemed most relaxed while eating and her capacity for food was beyond belief (accounting for her twenty–six pounds overweight). She expressed the fear that there would never be enough to eat.

Carmella's short attention span prevented her from learning new ways. She could not follow directions and had a pseudo–stupid quality. Anger and aggression were apparent in her shrieking and in the quality of her play.

At the same time Carmella was helpless and clinging. When she looked at animal puppets, she became terrified. For all these reasons, which revealed deep disturbance, Carmella was selected for TNG. The psychiatric report indicated "infantile behavior, depression, severe separation anxiety, and developmental lag." This slow development was intensified by severe problems in the home.

The psychologist's report placed Carmella in the low –average intelligence range. Her entire performance was on the level of a three year old. Her vocabulary was limited, and she did not know numbers, colors, or letters. The psychologist found her to be depressed and dependent, with strong drives and poor ability to control them. Carmella came across as a demanding, aggressive, annoying child, who wished to remain a baby rather than grow up.

Because her mother worked, Carmella was cared for in her early childhood by a psychotic, overweight father (two hundred pounds) who was very fond of her. But her father suddenly deserted the family when Carmella was two years old. Her mother had not told Carmella that her father was not returning. She reasoned that "it would make Carmella sad." This inability to communicate painful reality to a child is quite common. Our experience has shown that the bewilderment and confusion of not knowing is far more detrimental than the stark truth, which helps the child accept reality and prepares him for further growth.

Carmella's mother was ineffectual and could not offer her a sense of familial structure, controls, or any reasonable expectations. A soft–spoken, reserved, attractive woman, she functioned effectively in areas outside mothering, holding down a job as lab technician. Her feelings toward Carmella, the social worker found, were ambivalent. She still kept the child in diapers and bottle–fed her at the age of five. This over–intensive mothering was then negated by the fact that Carmella was never dressed attractively. And despite Carmella's evident weight problem, her mother filled her pockets with candy. This questionable family relationship was further complicated by the fact that Carmella's uncle, who had become a father figure, was stabbed to death.

Carmella's early sessions were turbulent. She rolled on the floor, shrieked if she couldn't have what she wanted, and bumped into children and objects as she galumphed along. Alternately, she would gather indiscriminate armloads of toys and stuff fistsful of crackers into her mouth. She did not pause long enough to enjoy either. It was clear that her need was the acquisition of things, and not the utilization of them.

Moving cautiously, the teacher–therapist expressed her acceptance of this need. Carmella had gathered all the dolls, dress–up clothes, and as many nursing bottles as she could hold. The teacher–therapist observed, "You like lots." Carmella smilingly nodded. The teacher–therapist responded, "So much to carry. Would you like a shopping bag to help?"

Carmella toted toys in the bag for many sessions. She was permitted to "play" this way as long as it didn't interfere with the rest of the group. The acceptance of this need was the starting point with Carmella. Her behavior had kept children and adults away from her. She was caught in a vicious cycle, wanting more and more and getting less and less. She could not grow until this infantile need was worked through.

One must always recognize the child's level of behavior and start from that point. When a teacher accepts and responds to the dependency needs of a child, the child's immaturities often become apparent. Many teachers are reluctant to have this happen, wanting the child to "act his age." However, this increase in dependency is often appropriate and necessary for a child like Carmella, who needed a gratifying relationship with a mothering figure. For reference to this theoretical concept, see Alpert (1963).

Carmella proved very hard to reach. Collecting armloads of toys, she was unable to respond to the teacher–therapist's overtures; she was off and running, elusive of contact. Despite this, the teacher–therapist kept offering suggestions that might help Carmella experience satisfying play.

Carmella: (racing about the doll corner) I drink from the bottle . . . (picking up the bottle and dropping it) I cook.
Teacher–Therapist: (picking up the baby doll) Cook for the baby?

Carmella took the baby doll and began to feed it the bottle. She filled the bottle in haste, shoving it in the doll's mouth.

Carmella: Baby wants more milk.
Teacher–Therapist: Does the baby ever get enough? Filled up?
Carmella: Never.
Teacher–Therapist: The baby wants more and more. She's a very hungry baby.

Carmella continued to feed the doll, and more and more water gurgled from its mouth. As the doll clothes became soaked, the teacher–therapist asked, "Does the baby feel cold when she wets?" Carmella felt the wet clothes. She repeated, "Wet," and then accepted a dry dress. As she proceeded to change the doll, she said, "Diaper." The teacher–therapist made a diaper for the doll.

Carmella: I be baby, you say baby to me.

Then she crawled like a baby, cooed, and climbed into the doll bed, sucking her thumb.

Teacher–Therapist: (patting Carmella) You want to make believe you're a baby. You are resting now . . . I'll help Ethan and then come back to you.

Carmella got out of bed and followed, crawling by her side, touching her skirt. The teacher–therapist again said, "It's fun to be a baby, to make believe." Carmella really smiled. Very much aware of the make–believe quality, she was never engulfed or lost in the play. This kind of nurturing experience enabled feelings of hunger and comfort versus discomfort to be brought into awareness. The doll play was important. She was out of touch with herself and her feelings, and was now experiencing them through the doll.

The baby play wove in and out of many of the early sessions. Carmella usually filled numerous bottles with water, sucked and fondled them, and lay in the doll's bed. Gradually she could leave this play and engage in age–appropriate activity. She alternated between the role of the baby and the five year old. Apparently the baby play offered enough satisfaction so she could throw off the baby cloak and demonstrate her real abilities. For example, she crawled into the doll's bed, made cooing sounds and said, "Say baby to me." Then, noticing the other children cutting and pasting, she said, "I want," and joined them. She was able to remain at this age–appropriate activity with some support from the teacher–therapist.

Carmella's reaction to the consistent support and approval of the teacher–therapist was often unexpectedly and dramatically displayed. She began to move out, relate, and use materials.

Carmella: (to Ethan who was huddled in a corner of the yard crying) Mary Jane is here.

Later Mary Jane (the teacher–therapist) told the group both of Carmella's concern and her attempt to help. Carmella, listening quietly, was so pleased with this positive description of herself that she could skillfully assemble three puzzles, demonstrating speed and accurate perception for the first time. This ability carried over into other sessions.

Another astonishing change was her willingness to use language. "Whaa dis . . . whaa dat," evaporated as the relationship took hold. Three– and four–word phrases emerged, and the pseudo–stupid quality was only apparent when Carmella became negativistic. By the end of the year, Carmella communicated feelings verbally: "Mother hit me for nothing." "I was sad when you didn't come."

Throughout the year Carmella went through many turbulent episodes. She had tremendous difficulty leaving the playroom and sharing toys, food, and her teacher–therapist. A meaningful relationship between the teacher–therapist and Carmella had to develop before she could begin to cope with these difficulties. By accepting her infantile play, the teacher–therapist started at Carmella's level and built from it. Playing ring–a–round–the–rosy and peek–a–boo were responses to her spoken and unspoken needs.

Leaving at the end of the session triggered Carmella into anger. Becoming highly excited, she would lose control and suck her thumb, only taking it out of her mouth to scream and stick her tongue out. Her behavior was frantic; she rolled on the floor, crawled under the table, and shrieked in a high–pitched, ear–shattering voice, upsetting the other children.

The teacher–therapist acknowledged to Carmella: "It's hard for you to leave. You'll come in two days. You're telling me you want to stay. When you're so excited you can't hear me and I can't help you—and I want to help you."

These words seemed to fall on deaf ears. During the next few months the teacher–therapist worked at tuning Carmella in to her desire to stay. The teacher–therapist physically comforted Carmella, reassured her that she would come again, and empathized with her difficulty in leaving.

In one session Carmella was angry; she screamed instead of talking. She grabbed a doll, put it in a chair with its back to the teacher–therapist:

Teacher–Therapist: The doll's not looking at me; she doesn't want to?" (Carmella nodded.) How come? (Carmella did not answer.)
Teacher–Therapist: Is the doll mad at me?
Carmella: Doll mad!
Teacher–Therapist: Doll mad! Does Carmella feel mad?
Carmella: Doll mad. Carmella mad.
Teacher–Therapist: Oh, maybe I can guess why. Did she want more crackers? (Carmella shook her head vigorously.) More toys?
Carmella: (yelling) No!
Teacher–Therapist: Was she mad because she always has to leave when she doesn't want to?
Carmella: Yes.

Now the teacher–therapist reiterated that this did make the doll and Carmella mad and sad.

Teacher–Therapist: Then the girl was screaming because she was mad.

Carmella: I scream and I scream.

Teacher–Therapist: And then what happens?

Carmella: I scream and scream and get all excited and Mommy gives me it.

Teacher–Therapist: It?

Carmella: Candy, toys.

Teacher–Therapist: (reminding Carmella) When you tell me like you just did now, then I understand and can help you.

A plan was evolved to allow Carmella to stay and help clean up for a few minutes after the sessions, which, surprisingly enough, the other children accepted. They seemed to understand and empathize with Carmella's difficulty in leaving. Bettleheim (1969) discusses the tremendous role of the peer group. In this instance, the children's understanding and acceptance was due to the certainty they felt that they would receive the same consideration of their own specific needs. When she began to manage better, she would ask to leave before being told it was the end of playtime. This adjustment lasted a few sessions, and then she was able to leave with the group. We felt that the difficulty at separation was related to her father's abrupt disappearance. Through the teddy bear she eventually played out her wish to "be in Colombia with her daddy."

Carmella's contacts with children grew from none at all to an occasional friendly gesture or phrase. When Ethan needed a cup at juice time, she graciously offered hers. On Carmella's birthday, Verna said she was scared because the lights were out for the lighting of the candles. Carmella ran and put the lights on. At a later session she said to Verna, in her first real interaction with another child, "Build with me." These interactions grew, and the play developed content.

Carmella and Verna played together with the mini–doll furniture and dolls. When friction developed over possession of a carriage, the teacher–therapist supplied a second baby carriage, enabling the two to continue playing. (The emphasis at this time was on the relationship and not on the ability to share.) At one point when Carmella took one of Verna's baby dolls, Verna hit Carmella, shrieking, "No!" Carmella hit Verna back. The teacher–therapist pointed out that Verna liked to play with Carmella but when Carmella did that "she didn't like it." The two girls continued to play together.

On one occasion, Carmella and Dominick enthusiastically cut out stars, triangles, and hearts using the cookie cutters and play dough, and served the group. Carmella's involvement in this kind of play and her increasing domesticity was paralleled by a change in her feminine identity. No longer a "blob," she began to enjoy dressing up, dancing, and mirror play. She commented on her teacher–therapist's lipstick, hair, and clothes.

Delightedly she clothed herself in a new, flowery, play skirt, scarf, necklace, and gold belt. She and her teacher–therapist looked in the mirror together. In response to "How do you look?" she answered, "Pretty." She spontaneously twirled in the skirt and then skipped (for the first time in TNG) toward the teacher–therapist, her hands outstretched. Her eyes sparkled, and her face was aglow with pleasure. Her teacher–therapist skipped toward her, their hands meeting. Carmella's icebox exterior had melted, her body was relaxed; she was graceful and responsive. Thereafter, she became interested in dancing with the tambourine and castenets and requested Spanish records.

Carmella developed a sense of herself. She gave up the role of the baby and began to take initiative. She found real pleasure in her accomplishments, and her use of materials became age–appropriate. Her scribbles progressed to drawings of girls with all the features included—even hair with a ribbon—but she still drew the mouth asking for candy and gum. Her vocabulary increased and her screaming subsided, as she became willing and able to articulate her requests.

She related with some warmth and friendliness, not only in the TNG room, but in her regular nursery room as well. She had become emotionally more accessible.

At the end of the year, Carmella was able to go on to first grade. However, because of slowness in learning, she was not promoted at the end of the year and repeated the grade. At this time she was seen in individual treatment because of the difficulty in school and her obesity.

Her second year of first grade was successful; she became interested in learning, had some friends, and her teacher felt encouraged by her emotional and intellectual growth spurt. During this year Carmella was seen once a week by the same teacher–therapist. Her basic conflict about growing up was further resolved. Carmella's mother became more cooperative after Carmella, in the presence of the teacher–therapist and her mother, said: "I'm fat, I'm a baby, no one likes me." The mother proceeded to help her to diet and allowed and encouraged some independence.

Depressed, Constricted, Withdrawn

Rhoda

Rhoda sat very quietly, staring blankly into space. Her large, brown eyes didn't blink and she didn't seem to hear her name being called. This sturdily built little girl, whose school attendance was sporadic, tried to cope with her nursery school experience by withdrawing into an impenetrable cocoon and rarely responding to attempts to engage her.

Her regular nursery teacher referred her to TNG because of this very slow adjustment to school and because she felt that there was real bitterness, as well as depression, in Rhoda's facial expression. Rhoda played only with boys, and even then there was a vagueness in her relating; she seemed "out of it." Her teacher reported a great deal of cursing and anger in her play in contrast to her usual withdrawn behavior.

Rhoda, a four–and–a–half–year–old Puerto Rican child, was the youngest of four children. Her father was out of the home and never mentioned; her mother had been known to social agencies for years because of truancy problems with the older children. She was also known to the project housing authority because of the disruptive parties she held and the incidents of malicious mischief which had taken place in her apartment. Its door was destroyed, windows were broken, etc.

The psychiatrist saw Rhoda as fearful and withdrawn. She would be sulking one moment and then bursting into a temper tantrum the next. She demonstrated extreme clinging and infantile behavior; she was anxious and extremely depressed. The overall impression was of a four–and–a–half year old whose clinging mutism, thumb-sucking, and tantrums were symptomatic of an unresolved dependency –independency conflict. Her fund of information was poor, as if no one had ever taken the trouble to teach her anything. The psychiatrist felt that a neutral, encouraging atmosphere in TNG, with an attempt to develop skills and form peer relationships, should be a primary goal.

The psychologist's report indicated an I.Q. score in the

average range (101) with a potential for somewhat higher functioning. Her lack of basic skills related to not being taught rather than a learning defect. There was a projection of eating themes, suggesting her need for nurturance at an early level of development. She tended to feel in danger, and her vivid fantasies were filled with destroying monsters. A consistent and dependable relationship with an adult was felt to be a primary need.

Working with Rhoda was extremely slow and difficult. Not only was she very withdrawn, but she had great difficulty relating, especially to girls and women. However, the crux of the problem lay in her sporadic attendance at the Day Care Center and, therefore, in the TNG group. She was present for only five of the first twenty–four sessions. The pattern of truancy, present in the older children, was clearly evident in the mother's handling of this four year old. The TNG approach to Rhoda was therefore complicated by her mother who had to be reached first, and motivated to send Rhoda to school. Although the social worker attempted to do this, it was only under threat of Rhoda's expulsion from the Day Care Center that the mother finally brought her to school more regularly. Rhoda attended fifteen of the next twenty sessions.

During the first sessions, Rhoda was dazed and passive, and often looked sleepy. She would begin the session by remaining at the table. After eating ten or twelve crackers, drinking two or three cups of juice, she would sometimes look around and watch the children. At other times she seemed oblivious to the room.

During one session, when Rhoda had finished all the crackers and juice at the table, and looked dazed, withdrawn, and tense, the teacher–therapist, feeling she would respond to physical contact, took her by the hand. "Let's find something you like." They walked around the room together as the teacher–therapist pointed out the dolls, the blocks, the play clothes, etc. Rhoda finally and hesitantly settled down with play dough and gradually became more relaxed. Toward the end of the session, she said, "I'm making a pancake." This was the first unsolicited verbal comment she had made.

In another session Rhoda would not respond to any attempt to interest her in material. She finally pounded clay, eventually putting a large pancakelike piece of clay over her face. The teacher–therapist was able to reach her with a peek–a–boo game. While removing the clay and putting it back, the dazed, unrelated look passed; and after a short time, Rhoda responded to John and Seth, who were making pizza out of clay, saying she didn't want their stupid pizza.

Rhoda's dazed, unrelated quality came and went. It was a kind of withdrawal which could be broken with infantile play, as the following session demonstrates.

Rhoda lay down on the table. Sue also lay down on the table. John and Seth got the doctor kit, pretending to give the girls shots. Sue was active in the game, pretending to cry, to be sick, to feel better; Rhoda was passive and didn't say anything. The children wandered off, Seth and John to the dump truck, Sue to the puzzles. Harry got the bubbles. Rhoda lay on the table, sucking her thumb, apparently not attending to anything going on in the room. The teacher–therapist put a folded blanket under her head and sat on the table, patting her back, occasionally talking to the other children. "Harry, blow the bubbles here so that Rhoda can see them." Harry blew the bubbles near her, but Rhoda showed no interest. In a few minutes, the teacher–therapist put a bright silk scarf over Rhoda's face saying, "Now you can't see the bubbles," and then, removing the scarf, "Now you can see them." Rhoda smiled.

At this point, John and Seth began to fight and the teacher–therapist left the table to help them. Rhoda scooted under the table; after two or three minutes, she threw a piece of wool at the teacher–therapist, who said, "Is it a little mouse throwing that? A little chipmunk throwing that?" Rhoda did not answer but gave a little squeak. She spent the next five minutes crawling around on all fours. John and Seth joined her under the table adding a blanket to make a tentlike structure. The teacher–therapist, trying to encourage Rhoda's activity and tie her in with the other children said, "The boys liked your game."

Rhoda's use of materials was very infantile and unimaginative for most of the first year. Pounding clay, rolling play dough, pouring water, and eating were her primary activities. By the end of each session she was more active and related, but then she would be absent for several sessions and the process would begin all over again. At this time the teacher–therapist, working slowly and almost nonverbally, had to be careful not to intrude upon what seemed to be a need for distance.

It was not until February that Rhoda began to smile as she entered the playroom. Yet her body tone and behavior were listless, characterizing her chronic depression. She still put her head down on the clay table, she still sucked her thumb. Her emotional quality had shifted from dazed and withdrawn to quiet and unenthusiastic. She was a little more aware and responsive in the room, and spent her time playing with very mushy play dough. She obviously enjoyed the tactile sensation, and began saying "gushy, mushy" as she smiled, repeating "gushy, mushy" to the other children who were hammering near her. (Her verbalizations were like those of a much younger child.)

The following session Rhoda began playing lethargically with clay, then actively tore it into small pieces. She placed the small strips of clay into a plastic container, filling it with water.

John: It fish? (All the children responded excitedly, coming over to see, and made fish to put into her container.)
Rhoda: (smiling) They like my fish!

This marked her first response to the group's reaction to her.

As Rhoda attended school and TNG more regularly, her relationship with the teacher–therapist slowly began to develop. It was a prolonged process. A flutter of a smile or an overt request were flickers of responsiveness to the teacher–therapist.

One day Rhoda, looking unkempt and sullen, walked around her classroom, randomly kicking at chairs. She didn't respond when the teacher–therapist greeted her.

Teacher–Therapist: (taking Rhoda's hand) You look like you have trouble.

Rhoda nodded yes.

Teacher–Therapist: Do you want to come to the play room or stay here? You tell me and it will be OK.
Rhoda: Come with you. (turning to Judy and Jean, her teachers, yelling) Fuckin' bastard!

Once in the playroom, there was no indication of the previous mood and she made it clear that she would not discuss what had happened. This inability to say what or who bothered her made it difficult to provide her with a feeling of being understood.

During this session, all the children but Rhoda became involved with the darts. Rhoda sat quietly munching crackers. She looked wistfully at the teacher–therapist and then quietly said, "I want something special." She and the teacher–therapist went to the closet door. Despite Rhoda's nonverbal message, "Don't intrude," the teacher–therapist acknowledged the incident in the classroom.

Teacher–Therapist: You were angry at Judy and Jean.
Rhoda: (completely ignoring the teacher–therapist's comment) I want that toy.

She chose a table game (the balloon game), and—over her mood—she and Sue became completely involved in the game, laughing and playing for ten or twelve minutes.

In the playroom her mode of functioning had changed. She could be drawn more easily into contact and her dazed withdrawn quality was evaporating.

At a slightly later session, when the teacher–therapist went for her in the regular nursery room, Rhoda was sitting with her finger in her mouth, apparently sulking. The teacher–therapist crouched down next to her and said, "Hi." Rhoda refused to look at her. The teacher–therapist stayed right next to her, and Rhoda finally allowed her to catch her eye and then spontaneously giggled. The teacher–therapist put out her hand saying, "Let's get the other children." Rhoda came happily but on her way out turned and stuck out her tongue at one of the children. In the playroom session she easily became involved with a woolly animal and seemed to have gotten over her mood.

Teacher–Therapist: How about sitting next to a friend?
Rhoda: Sue. (Rhoda sat down next to Sue at the mini–doll table but did not become involved in the play.)

Teacher–Therapist: Sue looks glad to have you next to her.
Sue: (getting up and selecting two dress–up outfits and
    turning to Rhoda) Play with me?
Rhoda: O.K.

She played passively, accepting the nursing bottles that
Sue had handed her, but refusing to dress up.

The content of her play remained meager, but she slowly
became part of the group activity. At another session
everyone sat at the table. Sue, John, and Seth talked about
the circus; Rhoda was silent. Later in the session, Rhoda
held the bear puppet, while Sue held the dog puppet. Both
children pretended the puppets were crying.

Teacher–Therapist: They're crying. What makes them cry?

Rhoda has her puppet fall down.

Sue: (as her puppet falls down) Help, help.
Seth: (entering the play with the policeman puppet) Now
    don't get excited.

Seth and Sue continue to play; Rhoda, playing by herself, repeatedly has the puppet fall down.

Teacher–Therapist: The bear falls down so much.
Rhoda: She takes dope.
Teacher–Therapist: And that makes her fall down?

At the next session, Rhoda spontaneously punched the
Superman punching bag. Asserting herself, she would not
allow anyone else to become involved, and stayed with
the activity for most of the session. She really seemed to

be enjoying her activity and the teacher–therapist enjoyed her activeness.

By March of the first year, her relationship with the teacher–therapist was more overtly expressed. Rhoda refused to go back into her nursery room and kicked at her teacher.

Teacher–Therapist: (taking her hand) Tell me, you tell me; then I'll know and Jean will know.

Rhoda: I need one more M & M. (as she and the teacher–therapist walked back to the TNG room) I want to stay with you.

Teacher–Therapist: You told me. I'm so glad you have a good time with me. I'll see you on Monday and we'll have a long time together, but now I have to go home.

Rhoda readily reentered her classroom.

Toward the end of the year, she began to talk in a more personalized way. "I cut my finger, and when I was crying, my mother put on a Bandaid." After Rhoda related this incident, the teacher–therapist suddenly realized that no one had ever seen Rhoda cry in the two years she had been in the Day Care Center. The distance she had put between herself and her feelings became even more evident as she began to talk more and allow herself freer expression. As this happened, her problem with her role as a five–year–old child became the focus of the time spent in the TNG room. She continued to play with Sue, almost always assuming a passive role. As the girls often used the Ritz Crackers in the game, Rhoda allowed Sue to feed her, figuratively and literally.

In May, Rhoda's mother was in the hall as Rhoda was being picked up for TNG.

Teacher–Therapist: Hello, Mrs. G. I'm Rhoda's special
teacher (Mrs. G. had avoided meeting the teacher–
therapist.)

Mrs. G. looked as if she didn't understand and made
no response.

Teacher–Therapist: Would you like to show your mother
your playroom, Rhoda?

Rhoda nodded and took her mother's hand. Mrs. G. followed the group into the room. She seemed uninterested
and distracted; she left quickly, without saying goodbye,
without letting the teacher–therapist talk to her.

Rhoda was absent from the next session. Whenever she
was out, her return to the regular nursery room was difficult
and her return to TNG was marked by some regression.
For instance, she might go back to making clay fishes and
not respond verbally. However, the duration of the regression was brief—usually not more than one session, and
sometimes not even a full session.

Rhoda seemed almost indifferent to the end of TNG
for the summer. She liked the turtle she was given, but
her affect was flat. At this point, the team felt that Rhoda
would benefit from a second year of TNG. During the
summer she was reevaluated; the psychiatrist found many
striking changes when she retested her. Rhoda entered
the test room spontaneously, without timidity; there was
no thumb sucking or clinging behavior. She was mute for
a short time, but then began to chatter in a more expressive,
appropriate way. She remembered the examiner, related
warmly, and seemed to enjoy the session. She moved with
facility and grace and her speech had developed considerably: there was less slurring and her articulation was better.

She had not developed greatly in the cognitive functions, and her drawings were immature, but she seemed ready to learn in a more formal, structured situation. Using the family constellation, her mini–doll play was concrete. She interrupted her play to talk about her friends at school, her favorite teacher (the teacher–therapist), and all the boys—John, Seth, Joey.

When the teacher–therapist first visited Rhoda's room after the summer, Rhoda looked quickly at her, averted her head, and did not respond to her "Hi." She was busily working on a puzzle and, with apparently no provocation except the teacher's greeting, she was indicating, by her attitude, "Leave me alone, don't talk to me."

However, as the morning progressed and the teacher–therapist sat quietly looking at her as she colored, the situation improved.

Rhoda: It doesn't look like you.
Teacher–Therapist: It's been a long time since I saw you.
Rhoda: I was at the farm.
Teacher–Therapist: Did you like that?
Rhoda: They got animals.
Teacher–Therapist: Oh.
Rhoda: When we coming to your room?
Teacher–Therapist: On Wednesday.

Once Rhoda was back in the TNG room, she continued to progress as if there had been no summer break. The sessions note more frequent play with other girls and the surfacing of Rhoda's attitude towards being a girl.

At one session Rhoda and Sue played together with dolls, filling the nursing bottles and feeding the dolls (instead of the usual—Sue feeding Rhoda). Rhoda, although playing a mommy role, insisted she was the brother. She also had new sneakers on and told the children that they were boy's sneakers.

Rhoda began to be clear and decisive in her choice of activities: "Let's play ball," using the bean bag with the teacher–therapist and imitating the Mets' catching and throwing. "I'm a Mets player." Columbus Day was coming and at table time the group talked about the holiday.

Teacher–Therapist: And they crossed the big ocean in three
   boats. The Nina, Pinta, and Santa Maria.
Rhoda: No. That's a girl's name.
Teacher–Therapist: Yes, that's right.
Rhoda: Oh, no.
Teacher–Therapist: The person who named the boats liked
   girls and gave the boats girls' names. I like girls.

Rhoda looked skeptical. The teacher–therapist smiled at her.

Sue and Rhoda spent a good deal of time in the doll corner. They often paired off and more opportunities became available for Rhoda to develop her feminine identification. For example, Sue became interested in brushing her own hair. This led to mirror play, beauty parlor play, and an awareness of the fun there could be in dressing up. The girls noticed the new aprons the teacher–therapist had made for painting and water play, and they became interested in sewing. There was one session when Rhoda became so involved with the sewing cards that she could return to the activity in spite of being interrupted by a fire drill. She stayed with the activity until it was completed.

At this point, Rhoda's attendance once more became sporadic and she now participated in creating excuses for her absenteeism. She claimed that she had been away at her 'gramma's' and then partially contradicted herself by saying that she had been "sick, very sick." But in spite of these absences, her friendship with Sue continued to solidify. They often walked down the hall with their arms around each other, played together for most of a session, and Rhoda seemed better able to accept herself as a girl. At Halloween, when Sue said she was going to dress up as a fairy, Rhoda chose to be Bat Girl.

During one session, Rhoda left Sue and came over to the teacher–therapist as if she had something she wanted to say. The teacher–therapist commented on her happy smile, while Rhoda crawled into her lap. But when the child was asked if she had anything she wished to say, she merely cuddled closer, shook her head, and a few minutes later went back to her game. The elusiveness of the girl was still strongly evident, even when she was relating in a happier and, for her, a much freer manner.

But the positive direction of her development was predominant. She had become more spontaneous and verbal. She chose toys depending on her different moods. Sometimes she isolated herself with the punching bag or other play material; at other times, she joined the group. After an absence of a week during this stage, Rhoda chose the punching bag to play with. Later, she traced the plastic bear and filled in the eyes, mouth, and belt with paste and glitter. She did not interact with the group, but her degree of withdrawal was much less than during the first TNG year.

Rhoda was out again for several weeks around Christmas time, and on her return she chose to ignore the teacher–therapist's greeting. She seemed neglected. Her hair was uncombed and she was dressed in summer pants and a light short–sleeved sweat shirt. While the teacher–therapist sat quietly near her, Rhoda played actively with Bob and Alex and seemed unaware of her presence. Suddenly Rhoda put her arms around the teacher–therapist, who said, "I'm glad to see you. I have your Christmas present. Would you like it now?" Rhoda grabbed her hand and started for the door. As she looked at the doll, Rhoda said, "I was sick so we didn't have Christmas." She smiled as she received her doll. During this session she played with Sue, but no regressive behavior was observed. Her verbal participation and ability to rejoin the group after being kept out of school continued to improve.

In March, for example, Rhoda told the group she had been out because her mother was sick.

Rhoda: The doctor came. She got pneumonia and the flu.
Teacher–Therapist: Who took care of you?
Rhoda: Jeannie and Marco did (her sister and older brother).

Later at table time:

Teacher–Therapist: Sue looks angry. What makes children angry?
Rhoda: When they don't share with me and hit me and some kids broke down my door and I got a new door a blue one and when I'm seven I can reach it.

Duane tried to interrupt Rhoda several times but managed to control himself.

Teacher-Therapist: Duane, that's what makes your teacher angry. Now it's Rhoda's turn. Then it's your turn.
Duane: When I'm in New Jersey and Wanda's friends come over and don't let me go with them and stick out their tongues and call me names.

Rhoda: Do they call you fuck?
Duane: No.
Rhoda: What?
Duane: Nothing.

Rhoda began to participate in a word story game. Different words written on slips of paper were put in a basket. Each child selected a slip of paper; the teacher–therapist whispered the word to the child who then told a story about it. Rhoda's word was "angry."

Rhoda: Once upon a time my sister took pills and she got in trouble and my mother got angry, man, because she would have to go to the hospital for taking drugs.

This new–found ability to verbalize and more openly reveal her life style permitted the teacher–therapist to help Rhoda deal with her world. At another session her word was "sad."

Rhoda: Once when my mother and daddy went out and when they came home my daddy ran away to Puerto Rico, but now he come back and he's at my granma's and I see him.
Teacher–Therapist: That was sad at the beginning when he was away, but then it was happy at the end.

Rhoda would now chatter away. She told about pleasant incidents in school—a party, a snowball fight in the yard. She became much more active and imaginative in her play, often telling Sue what to do and occasionally planning play and carrying it out. Rhoda and Sue talked together about taking the dolls out of the doll bed so they could get into it. Rhoda then acted on the idea, saying as she tossed the dolls, "All out, all out, we get in." Her play was becoming more imaginative and had a sequence to it. During a puppet show, Seth used the monkey puppet, basing his story on *Curious George*. Rhoda participated: "I own this show, pay your money, pay your money," (pretending to collect and count the money, "10—100—5. Now the show."

By the end of the second year, spontaneity and liveliness had become delightful and integral parts of her personality. She still preferred to play with boys and came to school dressed in a t–shirt and pants. However, there were many indications that she was more comfortable with her feminine identity. At the end of one session, for example, Sue, Rhoda, and the teacher–therapist danced to a rock record. Rhoda ran to dress up in the long, play skirt and took a quick peep at herself in the mirror. During another "tell a story" time, her word was "beautiful," and she told this tale: "There was once a little girl and she was happy because she had a telephone in her room. And she called a friend of hers. When she grew up she had a dress like Cinderella."

Her mother continued to keep her out of school, and the team felt, at the end of Rhoda's TNG treatment, that truancy would be a problem. Toward the end of May, the teacher–therapist met Mrs. G. on the street. Mrs. G. said Rhoda was out of school because she had the chicken pox. When Rhoda returned to school, she said, "I was at my granma's. It's fun. I don't like coming to school and taking a nap."

Although the gains Rhoda made were certainly gratifying and she had experienced a need–satisfying relationship with her teacher–therapist, it was frustrating to feel that the family situation was still so chaotic and destructive. Mrs. G. would not accept any kind of help. The public school which Rhoda was to attend reported that she had not been enrolled. Mrs. G. was keeping her out until she was six, the mandatory age for attendance. The public school was alerted to the problem and asked to step in rapidly, using whatever pressure they could to encourage regular attendance.

Sue

Sue, an aloof, whining, four year old, always seemed to be sad. Her bushy, tangled mass of curls, never cut or combed, gave her an ill–kempt, neglected air. Her lethargic, despondent appearance masked what could have been prettiness and grace. She never seemed to receive any enjoyment or satisfaction from toys or friends. The compassion evoked by her depression and passivity turned into annoyance growing from the frustration of her continued unresponsiveness. Her regular nursery school teacher felt that she was a possessive, spoiled child with a short attention span.

Nothing ever satisfied her—toys, friends, food. She continually whined, demanded attention, and sought quantities of materials that she never used. Her hunger for attention and acquisition indicated the emotional vacuum and deprivation she felt in relationship to her mother.

Sue's mother was a striking, bohemian–looking woman. She was volatile and quick to anger. She had little patience with Sue and even acknowledged her indifference and lack of interest, saying things like, "I should have looked at her drawings before I threw them away." Her own turmoil was great, so she had little capacity or time for understanding her daughter. Mrs. M., a white woman whose marriage to a black man was ending, described her husband as a "free–lance con man, who doesn't know the meaning of responsibility." Mr. M. apparently indulged his own interests, ignoring the family. He was playful with Sue, but often didn't show up when expected, leaving Sue inconsolably disappointed.

Mrs. M. accused the social worker who interviewed her of being nosey and prying, and was most reluctant to give any further information about her husband or herself. She felt anxious and uncomfortable about the responsibility involved in bringing up her child, and her behavior toward Sue was contradictory and confusing. She gave the child toys instead of attention. Her immediate response to any conference relating to Sue was defensive rage. She would vehemently deny any problem, saying, "They're crazy at Day Care," but at the same time, she was eager for Sue to participate in the TNG group, saying, "It would be good for her." When called because Sue had a throat infection, Mrs. M. came and took her to the clinic, but she was angry and abusive to Sue, the receptionist, and the doctor.

Sue was placed in the middle of a conflict between her mother and her teacher, a woman with whom Mrs. M. openly fought. Sue brought her own toys to school, but was unable to share them. She would spend the day hoarding the toys, tantalizing the other children with them, and getting upset if they were touched. The regular nursery teacher explicitly asked Mrs. M. to keep Sue's toys at home. Mrs. M. seemed to listen and understand the difficulties created, but repeatedly sent Sue to school with several toys anyway.

The teacher–therapist managed to establish a relationship with Mrs. M. by arranging special dance lessons for Sue. After this Mrs. M. became more accessible; eventually

an alliance of interest and concern developed. Mrs. M.
began to realize the impact of her ups and downs on Sue
and this insight helped their relationship. But even when
Mrs. M. felt comfortable and at ease, her thoughts flitted
much the same way Sue's play flitted. She would say, "The
small group's wonderful—everyone has noticed a change
in Sue. It's the dancing lessons!"

The psychiatrist described a fearful, apprehensive child,
overwhelmed by anxiety and afraid of being abandoned.
A consistent theme of emotional deprivation ran through
her play during the psychiatric examination.

Sue participated in TNG for two years. The focus was
on a warm, nurturing structure in which she might begin
to see herself as a nice, pretty child. It was hoped she
would use her intelligence and gain satisfaction from relationships.

For many sessions Sue was given, as much as possible,
all that she asked for. This helped her to experience being
heard and to feel that what she wanted mattered. As long
as there was some display of satisfaction on her part in
getting a variety of toys—even though she showed little
or no satisfaction in playing with them—this was kept up.
However, Sue eventually memorized all the toys in the
closet. She asked for them one after the other, displaying
her general lack of enthusiasm and restlessness. Then the
emphasis changed to limiting the toys, helping her enjoy
them, and learning how to play with others.

Sue's behavior in the playroom would initially take this
sequence: She would scribble indifferently on some paper.
Approached by another child with a jump rope, she would
immediately shout, "Go 'way." While this child, rebuffed,
went to play with a second child indicated by the teacher,
Sue aimlessly wandered to the game table, trailing her

fingers in the water basin as she passed it. She sat down and fingered the parquet blocks. Momentarily interested, she placed four blocks on the design paper. Then she gazed around the room looking for something else to play with.

Teacher–Therapist: You started a design; let's finish it together (handing her the blocks).

Sue completed the block design.

Teacher–Therapist: How does it look?
Sue: (with a pleased expression) Beautiful!
Teacher–Therapist: Who made it?
Sue: Me.
Teacher–Therapist: It's fun to finish things and see how nice they look.

Eventually, her domestic play added form and structure to the group play, but she was always the first child to become distracted. She used her high verbal ability to get the other children to assume the role of mommy while she was the baby. The theme of complete helplessness recurred in all her play, whether with the mini–people, the puppets, or even with the Superman punching bag. Haphazardly dressed, and uncombed, Sue entered the playroom looking exhausted, moving sluggishly. She sat near the mini–dolls, placing the mother in bed, and, holding the baby doll, she cried, "Mommy, Mommy, Mommy!" (Her voice was plaintive with a resigned, helpless quality.) The teacher–therapist said, "What can the baby do when the mommy doesn't answer?" Sue wandered over to the water table, moving physically and emotionally away from the teacher–therapist, indicating her desire not to be intruded upon.

During another session Sue again used the mother and the baby figures saying, "Mommy, Mommy, Mommy, Mommy, I'm speaking to you . . . (long pause—no response from the mother doll). I'm going to throw myself outside. (long pause) I guess nobody can't talk." Sue turned to the teacher–therapist saying, as she made the baby doll hit the mother doll, "She's angry!" Then she turned back to the doll play saying, "Mommy, how come you leave me!"

Because Sue communicated a need to keep her distance the teacher–therapist responded by cautiously waiting until Sue included her. It took a long time for Sue to trust her teacher–therapist; in many sessions she wandered away, shutting out the therapist, saying in different ways, "I'm not ready."

One day Sue was sitting alone in her regular classroom. She looked tired, angry, distressed. She had been crying and, according to her regular nursery teacher, had been the victim in a fight which she had provoked. Later, in the TNG room, she sat huddled at the table, tears still streaking her face.

Teacher–Therapist: (feeling Sue's misery) You look so sad.
Sue: I saw my daddy. (This is the first time Sue connected
    her unhappiness to this relationship.)

Sue got up and sat in her cubby far from the children and the teacher–therapist.

Teacher–Therapist: I know it's sad to talk about—that's
    O.K.—maybe another time.

Sue couldn't find anything that satisfied her, rejected any help from the teacher–therapist, and lay down in the doll's corner. The teacher–therapist verbalized her feelings for her: "You saw your daddy, and you had a fight in school—you're really feeling unhappy." But it took a long time for Sue to talk about her unhappiness.

A session later, when playing with Duane:

Duane: (throwing the bean bag at the mother and father bear) I mad at them. They mad. My mother don't want my father to live with us, but I do. My father lives with my grandma.

Sue: My mother doesn't want my father so he got someone else. (Her voice was flat; she sounded tired, almost uninterested.)

Duane: Sometimes I see my daddy. He's a lovely man. He likes me. He can walk, but when he run he shaky.

Teacher–Therapist: That's because he's sick.

Sue: I can sleep over.

Duane: I don't get to sleep over, but if I sleep over, I sleep with my father, not my grandma. Hold this, Sue (handing her a truck).

Sue turned away—her usual reaction to a friendly overture.

Teacher–Therapist: Maybe later Sue will say yes.

Duane: I'll be the daddy and the moving man.

Sue: O.K., but you go downstairs and go to work (constantly keeping her distance).

This incident clearly indicates the impact of the children upon each other. It also shows how resistant Sue was, because of her vulnerability, to allow the children or the teacher–therapist to intrude in such a painful area. When she finally included the teacher–therapist in her life, she dictated the role she wanted her to play.

Months later, Sue took the mini–mother, father, and

baby dolls. She plaintively said, "Mommy, Mommy, Mommy," then she took the baby doll and the toy couch and pressed them down on the mother's neck. She looked at the teacher–therapist.

Teacher–Therapist: What is the baby doing?
Sue: (ignoring the question) You be the mommy.
Teacher–Therapist: O.K., (taking the mommy figure) what does the mommy say to the baby?
Sue: No, you say the words.

The teacher–therapist, using the mini–mother, made oatmeal for the baby doll, singing to the baby as she cooked in the mini–kitchen, playfully feeding the baby doll. Sue cooed for the baby, saying, "Take me to the park! Take me to the park!" The teacher–therapist carefully dressed the mini–baby doll and wheeled her to the park, pretending to rock her in the carriage. When they returned home, bath–time was enacted, and the baby doll was kissed good night and put to bed. Then Sue said, holding the baby doll, "The baby listens to the good mommy."

The same pattern was followed in the puppet play. She often would initiate a puppet show, always choosing the baby, always crying "Help! Help!" Although the other children, using their doctor, fireman, mother, or father puppets, came to the rescue, Sue's "Help, help!" continued. However, when the initial change toward openness occurred in the mini–doll play, she was then more accepting of the help offered by the children in the puppet shows.

During this early "Help, help!" period, it didn't matter what material she was using. Once, while walking to the room, she finally said with some enthusiasm, "I'm going to play with the Superman punching bag." The teacher–therapist was thrilled at this sign of change in her play, expecting her to use it as a punching bag. But she got the bag and lay down on the floor yelling, "Help! Help! Superman, help!"

Gradually the content of her play changed and she was interested in having someone (teacher–therapist or children) play the good, helpful adult as she continued to play the baby.

Emotional changes were very gradual. Her fears of abandonment and of being disliked changed from a consistent "Nobody is there—help, help!" to "Let's pretend you love me—and are always going to love me!"

As Sue dramatically acted out her image about herself and her world, she also began to let her feelings show. When the children taunted her about her hair and her ill–fitting clothes, she would cry bitterly rather than passively withdrawing or sulking as she had previously:

Harry: (pointing to a picture on the wall of a child with blond, curly hair) You look like her.
Sue: (becoming distraught, crying, hitting ineffectually at Harry) I look like the girl with long hair.
Harry: You look like a rooster!
Teacher–Therapist: Sue doesn't like short hair; she thinks long hair is nicer.
Harry: (relentlessly) Rooster! Rooster!
Teacher–Therapist: (emphatically and firmly) You're making Sue unhappy and I want you to stop it.
Harry: Rooster! Rooster!

Sue stopped crying, while she listened to Harry and her teacher.

Duane: (who is usually the bully, teasing and belligerent)

Harry, shut up! I'll kick you in the balls! You look like a goat! (Rhoda, Sue, and Seth giggle.)

Harry: (stopped by Duane, turning to Sue) I'm sorry, Sue. You do look like the girl with the long hair.

(Children often sense areas of vulnerability and can tease cruelly.) Ignoring Harry, Sue went to the doll corner, then to the water table, then to the hammering set, unable to settle down. Rhoda asked her to play house. Sue smiled and for the first time played the role of mommy, handing Rhoda a bottle and covering her with a blanket. One can hypothesize that the support she had experienced from Duane and the teacher–therapist was deeply felt and significantly demonstrated by her change to the mother role in play.

Sue's sensitivity about her hair (which was really unkempt, tangled, and bushy) came up time after time. Then the teacher–therapist got a short, curly haircut:

Sue: It's ugly. You look like a rooster!

Teacher–Therapist: I had it cut short because I like short hair.

Sue: I hate it.

Teacher–Therapist: You don't like your short hair, but I like your hair and I like mine.

When Sue felt more positively about herself, the teasing lost its impact and she no longer reacted strongly.

Tiny bits of play began to reflect her changing feelings about herself. All the children sat at the table, cutting paper dolls and making clothes out of scraps of ribbon and fabric.

Sue: Look how nice. It's like me!

Sue got two dress–up outfits and asked Rhoda to play with her.

Rhoda: O.K. Got to wash my hands (she had been pasting).
Sue: We'll be sisters.

She went to the doll corner and put a doll under the cover. Harry ran over and grabbed the doll.

Teacher–Therapist: Harry, Sue is playing with it. Ask her
    if you can share it.
Harry: Let me have it!
Sue: You be the uncle and pretend you love me . . . and
    always love me (including him in the play, but refusing
    to give him the doll).

Sue poured a cup of coffee for the teacher–therapist. Duane came over and handed Sue a bracelet.

Sue: (putting on the bracelet) He always gives me things.
Teacher–Therapist: Sue, remember when you used to say,
    "Nobody likes me?"
Sue: That was long ago! (dressing up in play-clothes) Look
    at me!
Duane: Oooooh!
Teacher–Therapist: Pretty.

Seth entered the game, passively listening while Sue got married and bought a houseboat. The four children played cohesively for fifteen minutes.

Eventually Sue's puppet play became gay and she used stories and television programs for content.

Sue: (using the cowboys and horse) Now, ladies and gentlemen out there in TV land, listen to this song (singing a familiar song from Sesame Street). Now, clap!

Seth blew up the Superman punching bag. Sue ran to get a pot and spoon, coming back to Seth yelling, "Now, ladies and gentlemen, round one!"

As the children reacted to her sensitivity about her looks, they also reacted positively to her emerging gaiety. The children rested on the steps and a jumping game began spontaneously. The teacher–therapist quickly structured the game, having the children take turns. Sue had to hold the teacher–therapist's hand; eventually she jumped by herself.

John and *Seth:* (jumping up and down) Sue did it! Sue did it! (Sue looked pleased.)
Teacher–Therapist: Sue was afraid, but then she did it. Sometimes all children are afraid.

Basic to Sue's growth was her acceptance that the adults in school and the children would help her. Her trust developed very slowly, but progress is seen in the following example: After Sue had started dancing lessons, she misplaced her membership card. Her mother's rage brought both teachers and the assistant director to the scene. Sue's growing ability to cope with her world and see her mother's actions with some objectivity became clearly evident here. To the assistant director, she said, "Just listen to my mother yelling at me!" The assistant director managed to calm Mrs. M., and Sue could say at the next session, "She helped me."

She began to play dress–up, to comb her own hair, to wear play–clothes, and to enjoy dancing. The pathetic, despondent quality was rarely seen. She was now saying

she would be a mommy and a ballerina when she grew
up. It was a happier little girl who went off to first grade.

Infantile, Negative, Oppositional

Seth

Seth was referred to TNG by his classroom teacher
because of his infantile behavior. He is an attractive, well–
built, four–year–old black child. His large, expressive
eyes have an appealing quality and adults tend to respond
to him as they would to a much younger child. Whenever
he is near a teacher, his hand is on her knee or lap as
he leans against her. During a story he listens with one
hand touching his teacher's arm while he sucks on the
fingers of his other hand. His attention span is very short,
except when directly engaged in a one–to–one relationship
with his teacher. There is difficulty when he is asked to
leave one activity for another. At these times he will have
a temper tantrum; his teacher helps to calm him down
by holding him on her lap, rather than using verbal requests.

Seth is the youngest of four children; he has a fifteen–year–old sister, and two brothers, fourteen and twelve.
His parents are both working. Mr. D. works long hours
as a hotel porter and Mrs. D. works the midnight to eight
o'clock shift at the telephone company. Mrs. D. started
to work when Seth was eight months old. Although
extremely reluctant to give any personal details, she did
admit feeling rejected by Seth from time to time, usually
after a separation. Seth and a sibling would frequently

spend summers visiting his grandparents in Georgia for a week or so. When he returned home he would ignore his mother, call his older sister "mommy" and cry to go home to grandma. Seth had not really separated from his mother. This lack of individuation was basic to his inability to move without a mothering figure, (Mahler, 1968). His mother did not understand his rejection of her and felt hurt. She felt Seth's problems were the fault of the school. She did not remember any details of his early development, except for his hospitalization for pneumonia at ten months. She reluctantly gave her permission for Seth to be tested and seen in the small group. Mrs. D. gave the impression of being an angry, defensive woman who resented any intrusion into her own or Seth's private life. She did not become involved in any kind of counseling, and was difficult to deal with even in a telephone conference requesting permission for Seth to take a turtle home at the end of the TNG year.

The psychiatrist described Seth as an attractive, agile, right–handed, four–year–old child. He kept two or three fingers in his mouth most of the time. His coordination was good; his play rather unimaginative and concrete. She felt he was immature and unable to perform without the support of a nurturing, mothering figure. The psychiatrist felt he was anxious and the separation from the mother (at eight months when she went to work and at ten months when hospitalized) was a critical and painful period for him. His rejection of his mother after separation shows his attempt to deny painful feelings of loss with an "I don't need you" attitude.

TNG would focus on working out his separation anxiety, his defensive denial of feelings, and help him move into peer relationships and more independent behavior.

The psychologist found an I.Q. of 101. He felt Seth was hampered by an inability to abstract as well as extremely poor visual–motor ability. His grasp of a pencil was poor and he could barely approximate a circle. He appeared fearful and very infantile.

During the first TNG sessions, Seth was unobtrusive and caused no difficulty. He would sit quietly with three fingers in his mouth and do nothing. When invited into a game, he tended to say "I can't." He was resistant to the most enticing material (water play, bubbles, clay); when he did try to use the materials, there was very superficial involvement for fragmentary periods of time.

By late November the teacher–therapist noted:

Seth sat with his shoulders hunched, drawing his neck down. He shook his head from side to side saying, "I can't." He didn't seem to be angry, but the crayon fell from his fingers listlessly.

The teacher–therapist felt a familiar feeling of exasperation and frustration, as Seth sat and the three fingers went into his mouth.

It was this excessive inactivity, this seeming indifference, combined with a normal I.Q. score, that made everyone certain he could perform even though his negativism was constantly present.

After three months of TNG, the teacher–therapist felt certain that something was going wrong; it seemed as if a gigantic power struggle had developed. The teacher–therapist was saying, "I'm going to help you grow," and Seth was saying, "You can't make me." In this kind of power struggle the child wins, hands down; you can't *make* him learn or be involved. Many parents experience this kind of power struggle when toilet–training a child (you can't force him to make a bowel movement). In

December the anecdotal records were full of Seth's negative passivity.

When the teacher–therapist would ask Seth to match her white block with another white one, or her red with another, he would consistently reach for the opposite color. This deliberate or real failure was revealed in other types of simple matching play.

The teacher–therapist found herself not supplying acceptance and gratification, but rather falling into Seth's infantile pattern. For example, she anticipated his need to be helped with his coat, sweater, etc. (Later when Seth finally mastered buttoning his own jacket and proudly showed his mother, she said "That's good, now I don't have to bother with you no more." Seth promptly forgot how to button and "could not" learn to do it for several months.) A clear pattern of secondary gains began to emerge through extremely infantile behavior. At this point the teacher–therapist made an active decision to confront him directly, helping him become aware of his provocative behavior, which was hampering his learning and his relationships.

The children were drawing pumpkins with crayons.

Seth: I can't.
Teacher–Therapist: You like to make believe you can't do it.

At another time the children were pounding clay and making shapes.

Seth: I can't do that.
Teacher–Therapist: I think you can do it but you don't want to.

The children were playing a game to get M & M candies and name their colors.

Sue: I want red ones.
Harry: Give me yellow.

When Seth's turn came he stuck out his hand.

Teacher–Therapist: Tell me which color.
Seth: I don't know.
Teacher–Therapist: Remember last week you named one.
Seth: Blue.
Teacher–Therapist: I don't see a blue candy; what else
    is there?
Seth: Brown.
Teacher–Therapist: (enthusiastically) Yes, it's brown. Here
    you are, 1, 2, 3, 4, 5 brown ones!

He would annoy his nursery school teachers with this type of negative behavior. To make him aware of the anger he was provoking, the teacher–therapist would say, "When you make believe, you don't know it gets people angry." Children often sense the angry reaction they get from an adult and it is important to let them know clearly what is happening.

The teacher–therapist was ill and missed three sessions; when she returned, Seth acted out his sense of rejection. For the first time he was reluctant to greet her. This re–enactment of the behavior his mother had experienced —this reaction to separation—wove in and out of every session.

When the teacher–therapist entered Seth's room, he was sitting quietly, holding a picture book. As soon as he saw her, he put his fingers into his mouth; he avoided eye contact and her greeting. The teacher–therapist sat down quietly near him. In a few minutes Seth extended his hand. She smiled at him. "Hi, Seth, let's get the other children."

The children in the other room were not ready. The teacher–therapist sat down. Seth ignored the other chair and sat on her lap. Cuddling like an eighteen month old, he seemed to accept the absence and return of his teacher–therapist, and came willingly to the playroom. During the play session in the room, Seth and John interacted more than they had previously. There were strong elements of sibling rivalry in the play for both boys. John took the plane Seth was holding. Hoping Seth would stand up for himself, the teacher–therapist said, "You had it and John wants it too. You figure it out."

Seth didn't answer but threw the toy at John, who stopped crying. Then Seth threw himself on the floor and imitated Jeff's behavior exactly; John began to play with the toy. Seth seemed content and lay on the floor watching John. A little later the two boys spent about ten minutes playing with a ball. It was the beginning of interaction; even the negative interaction was a step toward socialization.

For the next several sessions Seth continued to avoid eye contact or acknowledge the teacher–therapist's presence when she first entered the room. Although it had seemed in the previous session that he had accepted her absence, apparently he had not. For example,

Rhoda: (running to Seth) Phyllis is here!
Seth: (looking at the ceiling) Where?
Teacher–Therapist: (playfully) You're teasing.

Seth did not respond; he looked away.

Rhoda: Let's go.

Seth shook his head.

Teacher–Therapist: You're telling me you don't want to
    come now. Later?
Seth: Yeah.
Teacher–Therapist: Joan will bring you when you tell her
    you're ready.

His regular classroom teacher brought him in about fifteen minutes before the period ended. He was smiling
as he entered the room, but then he calmly and deliberately
knocked down three chairs, the doll furniture, and every
toy in sight. He would not join the group at game time
and then defiantly hid under the table, refusing to leave
with the rest of the group. The teacher–therapist went about
straightening the room and talking to Seth, who remained
under the table. "You're really upset—can you tell me?"
There was no response from Seth. At this point his regular
nursery teacher came into the room and he left with her.

The teacher–therapist returned to Seth's room half an
hour later for a conference with his teacher. Again, Seth
looked at the ceiling, not acknowledging her presence. The
teacher–therapist said, "I know you're making believe you
don't see me, but I see you, and I like you." There was
no reaction from Seth.

Before the next session, Seth was sitting alone out in
his cubby. The teacher–therapist crouched next to him.

Teacher–Therapist: I think you were upset last time
    because I wasn't here and that was hard for you.

Seth kept three fingers in his mouth, would not look up,

and showed no signs of hearing.

Teacher–Therapist: Do you remember when you made
  believe you didn't see me?
Seth: Yeah.
Teacher–Therapist: I really wanted to come to see you,
  but I was sick.

This brief contact enabled Seth to come with the group.
During the session, Seth used the doctor kit, wanting the
teacher–therapist to be the patient. He refused to accept
a doll or another child as a substitute. His play during this
session was far more mature than before and had more
content. During story time, when a story was told about
a newborn baby, he spontaneously said, "My sister's going
to get her a new baby." (This was not true.) At the end
of each page, the children were asked to contrast what
they could do with what the baby did (slept in a crib, took
a bottle). Seth laughed and seemed to enjoy the "joke"
aspect of the comparison. The other children were really
laughing and enjoying naming the things they could do
that babies could not do. For the first time he matched
M & M's and picked a yellow one in response to "Find
a yellow one like this one." The teacher–therapist said,
"I'm glad you played the game with us." It was very difficult
to use a judicial amount of praise with Seth. He did so
little that the tendency was to overreact to anything he
did do.

The teacher–therapist felt Seth was now re-enacting
separation anxiety and dropping the pseudo–stupidity for
short periods of time. Her absence had seemed to focus
his behavior more clearly on the separation aspects of his
problem.

At the next session Seth suddenly threw himself on

the floor as the group was walking to the TNG room. The other children ran ahead, bursting into the room. A second teacher–therapist was there and settled them down. When Seth entered, he knocked over a puzzle, took the egg beater, and used it to knock over almost all the water equipment. The teacher–therapist said: "I can't let you do that even though you feel like it." He began to calm down and allowed himself to be led to the table. He "played" with some carpet scraps, making a road, and seemed relaxed for the rest of the session.

The following session began again with a huge screaming and crying tantrum. The teacher–therapist responded, "O.K., Seth. You have two more minutes to cry and then it will be time to stop." (After a pause) "Now it's time to stop." (He did.) Once in the room, he again began throwing toys. "I can't let you throw those things, but you can throw the dart." Seth grabbed a dart, aimed, and succeeded in hitting the target. He was then able to plant his seeds and play "bus" with John and Sue. He left with a friendly smile as the teacher–therapist said, "I'll see you next time."

But next time he again refused to come, even with his regular nursery teacher. The team decided to have the teacher–therapist remove herself from the battleground, and assume a more neutral position with him. On the thirty-ninth session, the other teacher–therapist brought him to the door of the playroom and dealt with his tantrum, until he eventually entered the room by himself, disregarding her suggestion to knock on the door. He still pretended he couldn't. He finally opened the door and came in himself. He spotted the circular plastic building cylinders.

Seth: How do you work it? (John tried to show him.)
Teacher–Therapist: Seth can figure it out. (The dependent

child is often overwhelmed by the feeling he needs someone every minute. It is very easy to feed this dependency by anticipating and infantilizing him, instead of allowing him to experiment on his own.)

Seth did figure out the game and had a pleasant session with no incidents.

The following session, Seth again refused to come to the playroom. The other teacher–therapist and his regular nursery teacher tried to bring him, but he screamed and kicked. It was decided to step out of the power struggle and not force him to come. At the end of the group session, the teacher–therapist approached Seth in his nursery room:

Teacher–Therapist: Do you want to water your plant or shall I do it?
Seth: Me.

In the playroom he wanted to stay and play with the toys.

Teacher–Therapist: You missed your time in here. If you want to come next time you tell Joan.
Seth: I want to.

For the next few sessions Seth again refused to come. He was reassured that when he decided to come, everyone would be glad. His teacher found him to be more difficult in the classroom. She said he cried, was more unhappy, and kicked out with little provocation. Children who are extremely passive and quiet will often go through an acting–out period as they become somewhat freer. This is the most difficult period for the parents and teachers working with the child. As much support as possible should be given to the regular teacher when this sort of thing occurs. The teacher–therapist continued to greet him and reassure him about his place in the group.

On March 25th, the forty-fourth session, Seth came quietly to the group with a friendly smile, after nearly two months of difficulty.

Teacher–Therapist: Hi, Seth, are you coming today?
Seth: Yes.

In the room he was actively engaged with trucks, water play, and feeding the dolls baby bottles.

Seth never again acted out in relation to coming to the room. In the next four sessions he returned to where he was before the acting–out had begun. He and John developed a close, exclusive relationship, with many competitive aspects. Sharing toys, friends, and the teacher –therapist was the focus for the next few months.

There wasn't enough juice for all the children and Seth went to the kitchen for more juice. John had a tantrum, crying that he wanted to go to the kitchen, too.

Teacher–Therapist: I know that you like to go and you will, another time. You like to do the same as Seth.

John continued to cry for a short time and then became involved with the pine cones. Later, John and Seth were taking turns with the one dart, which was broken. Suddenly, both boys were screaming, "It's my turn!"

Teacher–Therapist: (holding the dart) What do we do when two boys want the same toy?
Seth: O.K., go ahead. (The two boys went back to the game.)

Sue joined the game and the identical thing happened between Sue and John.

Seth: (holding the dart) What we do when you two want it? (This demonstrated Seth's beginning identification with the teacher–therapist.)
Sue: He's the teacher! He's the teacher!
Teacher–Therapist: Seth's learning about turns.

Later that day, as the teacher–therapist was leaving the building, she called to Seth who was playing in the yard.

Teacher–Therapist: Bye, see you Tuesday.
Seth: (climbing on the tire he was rolling) Give me a big kiss.

The teacher–therapist leaned over and kissed his cheek. He waved and scampered away.

There were other sessions when Seth, in his exclusive friendship with John, would not let anyone else join their games. He was more concerned with keeping children out than with having fun. He would often have a tantrum when another child participated in the play. By April, he began to play with the other children in the group, but he always played the role of the baby. When the group dramatized *Goldilocks and The Three Bears* he always wanted to be the baby. The group was extremely tolerant of his demand and always relinquished the role to him.

Although Seth was consistently taking the role of the baby in play, it was becoming more and more play rather than his life style. He also showed some concern over the other children's attitudes. Sue played with the nursing bottles. Seth seemed to be anxious; he tugged at the teacher–therapist, pointing to Sue.

Teacher–Therapist: Sue is playing she's a baby. It's a game.
Seth: She's the mommy (her usual role).
Teacher–Therapist: Sometimes she plays mommy.

At table time, we were talking about the weather. Seth answered all the questions, almost challenging Jeff's unquestioned leadership.

Teacher–Therapist: Is it hot or cold outside?
Seth and *John:* Cold. Freezing.
Teacher–Therapist: What do we wear on a day like today?
Seth: Me! Me! Let me!
Teacher–Therapist: John tell me one thing, and then Seth
    tell me one thing.
John: Coats.
Seth: Boots and gloves.

There were other indications that Seth was moving away from babyhood. Sue suddenly began bullying him into being the daddy in her games rather than the baby, and one day, when she accidentally spilled her juice, Seth said, "You like a little baby."

His play became less concrete and more involved. On one occasion when Sue and Seth were playing with the mini–people for an extended period, they evolved complex roles. Seth began by trying to zoom a fire engine into the mini–house. The teacher–therapist handed him a police-man and fireman.

Sue: Cars can't do that. (Seth walks the policeman to the
    house.) Did you bring me a present? Am I going to
    a party?
Seth: I am the policeman. I'm coming to your house.

Sue: (using the mother figure) This man is hurting my little girl.

Seth: (using the policeman) Why are you doing that?

Sue: (taking the male figure) O.K., I'll stop.

Later they loaded all the furniture and people into a dump truck and played at moving day.

Seth seemed to accept the end of TNG for the summer with little difficulty. The children were all excited about the turtles they were to take home and care for. They were also expecting postcards from the teacher–therapist. All of the children in this particular group were to be seen for another year beginning the following September. Over the summer they were re-evaluated by the psychiatrist and the psychologist.

The psychiatrist found that the infantile, "shy" quality in Seth was gone when she retested him. He was more capable of relating and was not actively oppositional. In contrast to the first testing situation, he seemed to be enjoying himself. The report noted: "Finger sucking, so prominent last time, was not observed even once. Speech showed considerable improvement with no noticeable articulation defects. He still made errors on colors, but knew most of them. He could now count to ten and identify most of the numbers, but he still had great difficulty with letters. His visual–motor perception was poor and represented a slight maturational lag. However, he seemed more able to learn and has benefited greatly from the TNG experience. There is no doubt, though, that he can profit from an additional year of TNG."

The psychologist found a nearly identical I.Q. score when Seth was retested (100, compared to 101). He noted a dramatic improvement in the ability to verbalize concepts,

but stressed that Seth's withdrawn behavior had initially
hampered his overall performance. Seth's rote memory was
relatively poor; he was somewhat inattentive and distract-
able. On the other hand, in tasks where he would apply
foresight and planning, his performance was particularly
good. Perceptual–motor coordination remained immature
and inadequate. The psychologist recommended another
year of TNG to help Seth express aggressive fantasies and
to experience his growing intellectual competence.

As the teacher–therapist entered the play yard after the
summer, Seth greeted her with a flying hug, yelling
"Phyllis!" across the yard. He then looked somewhat
embarrassed, and went back to playing with Abraham.

During this second year, he attempted many new learning situations. With great pride, he mastered rope jumping.
He not only memorized the simple *Touch Me Book,* but
he expressed curiosity as to how it was made. He proudly
"read" it to the group or to a single child many times.
He participated in group discussions and was able to convey
his own feelings, as on this occasion, when the children
were asked what made them sad.

Sue: When my mother spanks me.
John: When my brother won't play with me and I got
    nobody.
Seth: When the kids won't play with me.

At another session, Seth blew up the Joe Palooka punching bag with some support, even though he said "I can't"
as he was doing it. Then he really punched the bag around.
Later in the session, the teacher–therapist used a puppet
for each child, and dramatized Seth's behavior.

Teacher-Therapist: I can't do it—whooo, whooo—I can't

do it, I can't blow up the punching bag—whooooo! (the rest of the children chimed in, "Oh yes you can, oh yes you can").

Seth: Do more! Do more!

As the year progressed, the notes on the sessions indicated Seth's growing mastery of his world, his more complex use of both speech and materials. The following incident took place one spring day when Seth and Duane wore the same sweater.

Duane: We look like brothers.

Seth: I have two brothers.

Duane: I got a hundred and five sisters.

Teacher–Therapist: Duane thinks it would be nice to have a brother or sister.

Sue: I have a cat.

Seth: Paul, just watch TV and don't bother my trains or nothing.

Duane: My brother would take you out when your mother's too tired. My mother takes me out with my skates and bike.

Sue: My mother's tired.

Seth: My brother's so strong he can lift those . . . what do you call it?

Duane: The world?

Seth: No.

Duane: A building?

Seth: Barbells, I can lift one.

Duane: I got a hundred brothers.

Seth: Man!

Seth was hammering and sawing, as Reggie's teacher dropped him off. Reggie started to cry immediately and the teacher–therapist indicated to him, using the example of other children, that it was sometimes hard to do new things.

Teacher–Therapist: Remember when Seth didn't want to come to the playroom?
Seth: Yeah, man!
Sue: He had tears coming out of his eyes.
Teacher–therapist: My special job is to help children feel happier.

At juice time Seth said, "I have a story to tell," and proceeded to tell it: "There was a truck and another truck and they were trying to have a race and one truck flew up on a mail truck and turned over and the other truck turned over. And my brother ran and they used a chain to pull and the cops came and we watched and an ambulance came." (This was based on a real incident.)

One day when the teacher–therapist was late getting to school, Seth held her hand and said, "I was worried about you." This ability to express concern, and at the same time accept the teacher–therapist's belated presence, was a tremendous step for a child whose previous mode of dealing with separation fears was complete denial.

By the end of the second year of TNG, Seth's whole body tone had changed. He jumped, ran, climbed, and threw a ball with a sense of freedom and enthusiasm. The limp, dragging quality was rarely present.

He still tends to be a follower, but actively enters into games and activities. He asks for specific toys and verbalizes demands, needs, and fears. Now he can tell a story, contribute to group discussions, and hold his own in peer relationships. His teachers say he is no problem in the large classroom and his mother noted that he was easier to manage in the home. The team felt that this new Seth, able to cope with his feelings and his world, could now move on to first grade.

Aggressive,
Volatile,
Poor Impulse Control

Duane

Duane was a handsome, powerfully built, four–year–old black child. While he teased, punched, and bullied his peers, he would look warily around the room to make sure he wasn't caught. His delight in producing (almost instinctively) shrieks and tears in the children erected a barrier; both adults and children kept their distance from him. A perceptive, bright child, he was channeling his energies into destructive behavior. He misused his awareness of his environment and his ability to verbalize and conceptualize, and he seemed well on his way toward insurmountable difficulties. He had almost accepted being a loner and never having friends, but he was totally unaware that his own behavior was causing his isolation.

Every time the teacher–therapist entered his nursery room for the TNG children, Duane would insistently ask, "When ya gonna take me?" A place for Duane in the TNG did not become available until he was five years old.

The angry, defiant child is often seeking help, (Martin Kohn, 1965). Duane's insistent whine was attention–seeking and competitive. In spite of its annoying provocativeness, it was also an ingratiating plea for help.

His diagnostic workup indicated overwhelming anxiety, with fear of abandonment and physical destruction.

Duane's unresolved fears resulted in such inner turmoil that he could not learn; his distractability seemed to account for his low–average I.Q. score. His aggressive fantasies were of crocodiles and whales eating up people; he saw his mother as engulfing him.

His family life, like that of many aggressive, belligerent children, was chaotic and traumatic. His father was a drug addict who suffered brain damage from an overdose. Duane had witnessed convulsions and physical fights between his parents, and had been used as a pawn in the highly charged battles. Ultimately the police removed his father to Bellevue Hospital. The irreversible brain damage left him unable to work and in need of constant care. The horror with which Duane and others like him live can never be fully communicated. Expecting him to conform to a classroom situation without special professional help is unrealistic.

Duane's paternal grandmother was caring for his father when Duane entered the TNG. Duane longed for his father, and his mother complicated the situation by promising "they would all live together soon." Mrs. Green's attractiveness and competence in holding a receptionist's job belied the frightened, angry, defenseless woman who could not face feelings or reality with her child. She expected him to be a "strong, brave man," never to cry, or to be afraid. Duane's acceptance of this role was dramatically illustrated when his nursery school teacher went around the circle of children asking what they wanted to be when they grew up. Duane answered, "A daddy for my mommy." His mother never set limits and her discipline was erratic and violent. Children who expect immediate gratification and whose impulsiveness is indulged with no setting of limits remain on a primitive level and have difficulty developing self–control.

There were many instances when she completely ignored Duane's transgressions in the Day Care Center. Once, just as she was picking him up, he bloodied a little girl's nose. Mrs. Green appeared completely indifferent and told Duane to "go get his jacket." At another time, while the mothers were participating in an arts and crafts session, Duane annoyed the other children and the mothers by grabbing the glitter, the stars, and the glue from everyone. Again Mrs. Green remained oblivious. This behavior illustrated the mother's negation of her role and Duane's reaction to it.

The establishment and reinforcement of limits was constant and unremitting. Duane's time in the playroom was focused on teaching him which of his needs were legitimate and could be met, and which were not permissible and would not be tolerated. Duane was forced to leave the room when nothing else worked. He had to learn that his behavior would have an effect on the children and on the adult who cared about him. Beneath a smiling mask, his aggressive hostility continued to emerge but became more verbal and less physical. After giving Rhoda a nursing bottle he said, "I put Ajax in it so she'll die." At another session Duane hit Sue with a book.

Teacher–Therapist: Duane, what would you do if someone hit you with a book?
Duane: Kick him in the balls.
Rhoda: Tell him to stop.
Seth: Tell the teachers.
Sue: Cry.
Reggie: Hit him.
Teacher–Therapist: What do you think I should do?
Reggie: Put him in a chair.
Seth: Say "STOP IT!"

Duane: Kick him in the balls.

Rhoda: Send him out of the room.

Teacher–Therapist: Duane, they're telling you they don't like it, and I'm trying to help you stop.

Mid–year, a chance remark by his teacher–therapist demanding control of him became a crutch which he used dramatically to develop his own control.

Teacher–Therapist: I really mean it, Duane, you can't kick her.

Duane: My mother don't mean it.

Teacher–Therapist: She doesn't?

Duane: She say, "Take out the garbage," and I just stand still and then she say "Never mind."

Teacher–Therapist: But I really mean it.

At the next session, when Duane had to be stopped from pinching Rhoda, he startled the teacher–therapist by saying, "You didn't say 'I really mean it.'"

Because he was so bright, he used this phrase to demonstrate both his awareness of his behavior and the adults' expectations, and also to help maintain his own control. He became aware of what was acceptable behavior and began to seek approval for it, saying, "Tell Florence (his regular nursery classroom teacher) how good I manage."

Working with Duane was an exhausting, frustrating experience. He needed consistent, firm controls and the freedom to be a little boy who could express feelings of fear and loneliness. The team felt that his aggression was a response to his repressed fears. If he could verbally respond to, "What do you do when you're afraid?" there was a chance of helping him develop other modes of coping with fear. Unfortunately, Duane's insistent denial persisted through most of the year. He maintained a smiling exterior and an aggressive, belligerent, cursing, disruptive behavior pattern.

For example, one day when his teacher–therapist was entering the nursery room for the five TNG children, Duane knocked over the juice as he shot up from the table and kicked over two block structures in his haste to be first to reach his teacher–therapist. As the group left the nursery room he knocked a younger child down and was stopped from kicking him only by the adults' intervention. The whole episode took less than three minutes. Duane seemed oblivious of the impact of his behavior. His nursery school teacher handled the immediate disruption while the rest of the group waited for Duane to clean up the juice and stack the blocks.

Once in the playroom, he vaulted over the block cabinet and leaned out the window saying, "I'm running away."

Teacher–Therapist: I won't let you run away . . . you're very upset today.

Duane: Who made a fart? (dodging)

Sue: Stop with that farting business.

Reggie: Yeah, fart, fart, fart!

Duane: I like to make people laugh.

Teacher–Therapist: You like to make people laugh so they won't know how upset you are inside.

Duane angrily demanded the darts at this point. His play with them reduced some tension and eventually enabled him to join the group. However, he was just on the maintainable level. Duane strongly resented and resisted any attempt to explore his frequently frantic behavior. For many months, the effort to help him become aware that what he was saying and doing were closely connected to his feelings seemed ineffectual.

At this point, Duane's mother was living with her white lover and Duane was no longer allowed in her bed. On weekends he stayed with cousins in New Jersey, further intensifying his rage and fear of abandonment. This triggered his explosiveness.

Duane: Some white people stink.
Teacher–Therapist: Who?
Duane: Pat and Carey.
Teacher–Therapist: Oh, they stink?
Duane: They got a bad smell when you get near them.
     No brown or black people got a smell.
Teacher–Therapist: You're telling me you don't like them.
Duane: They sure got a stink.

Duane obscured his real feelings with barrages of this type of hostility. The desperation and anger he experienced and the conflict he had to cope with made working with him difficult. Each week the reality of his daily life overwhelmed him.

Duane's tough–guy façade melted almost imperceptibly over the year. The first indication of any growth was his change in role–playing. A favorite activity was dramatizing a familiar story with puppets. In the beginning, Duane always fought for the role of the father in *Goldilocks and the Three Bears.* Later in the year he suddenly began demanding the baby bear puppet. The change in choice of roles was the first indication that he might drop his tough façade and allow little boy feelings and reactions to emerge.

About this time, he cried bitterly when one child said she wouldn't be his friend, indicating that friendships were now part of his world and expectations.

Although he continually denied being afraid, he began to relate frightening incidents. For example, during a session when he was teasing and baiting the other children, the attempts to discover what triggered this behavior finally paid off, and he began to reveal himself.

Teacher–Therapist: When a boy acts like that I think something is bothering him.

Duane: No—(long pause) Hawkeye and Poopie drove me home (talking about returning from New Jersey).

Teacher–Therapist: Did they tease you?

Duane: No, they drove me home. They like me. They said there was a ghost in the house but I wasn't scared. I just stood straight (imitating standing rigidly).

Teacher–Therapist: I think that would scare a five year old.

Duane: No—(long pause). If I got lost I wouldn't be scared—I would walk for two whole days and nights till I found my mother.

Teacher–Therapist: Sometimes it's hard to be away from your mother.

Duane: No, we can go out and play by ourselves and go to the store and—and it's just around the corner.

There was a question here as to whether Duane was again denying his legitimate need of his mother, or moving towards a healthier, less helpless feeling. It was only toward the end of the year that Duane was trusting enough to disclose his deepest unhappiness.

Teacher–Therapist: When you act so wild I know you're thinking about something. Is there something you're thinking about today? (long pause) Did you go to New Jersey?

Duane: Yeah—(long pause).

Teacher–Therapist: Do you still see your father?

Duane: Yeah, he promise he come live with me ... he
   promise.
Teacher–Therapist: What does your mother say?
Duane: She don't want him.
Teacher–Therapist: Did she explain about that?
Duane: She don't want to! When my father was home in
   the living room playing records—and he beat me
   up—and when my mother come home—I say he beaten
   me up—and they go in the kitchen and fight and scream
   and then he left.
Teacher–Therapist: Duane, fathers sometimes hit children;
   and your father didn't leave because of that. He left
   because he and your mother didn't get along and
   because he was sick.
Duane: He still shaky. Everyone has a father. I want my
   father.
Teacher–Therapist: It's a hard thing for a five–year–old
   boy to understand.
Duane: He's a lovely man.
Teacher–Therapist: It's nice that you can see him and you
   know he loves you wherever he lives.

When he was free enough to allow feelings of grief
over the significant loss of his father's presence, he no
longer had to fall back on primitive measures of defense
such as feeling nothing and denying the pain of loss.
(Fraiberg, 1959). As less energy went into denial, he was
able to communicate more, and his impulsive, uncontrollable acting out lessened. The teacher–therapist could praise
him for his occasional, creative ideas. He began to play
for short periods and his need to be tough, strong, and
masculine was used in games: training like a prize–fighter
with a jump rope; playing tug–of–war with the children;
boxing with the Joe Palooka punching bag, or demonstrat-

ing his agility in games of follow–the–leader. It became easier to reinforce his growing desire to play with other children and to be accepted by them. At the end of the year, he proudly showed off how he could write numbers and the alphabet, and his interest in learning emerged.

Duane entered a Catholic school's first grade in September after one year in TNG. Many of his problems were unresolved; his impulsiveness and tendency towards aggression still existed. Once he was drawn into the conventional school setting, the TNG program was no longer available to him.

Individual treatment with a male social worker was made available so he could solidify his gains and work towards further resolution of his problems. But TNG did supply an important service for Duane and his mother. By the end of the year, he was less defensive, anxious to establish peer relationships, and trusting enough to enter into a therapeutic relationship. His mother knew more about him and was more comfortable using the Hudson Guild's Counseling Services for herself as well as for him.

Terry

Terry was referred to the TNG by the director of the Day Care Center who described him as "chronically angry and liable to lash out if he is crossed. He resents controls and routines are difficult. He is easily distracted. He does not have friends."

Terry was a five–year–old child whose enraged, disruptive behavior resembled Duane's. His blazing anger and inability to accept limits sprang from his identification with an immature, violent, jealous, frightening father. His mother had his father thrown out of the house. Terry was antagonistic and assaultive, caught in the chaotic marital strife. He was brighter than Duane, his understanding and comprehension falling into the eight–year–old level; his overall testing was in the bright–normal range. He was also emotionally accessible—and therefore able to use insights—and did not use denial as a major defense. Although initially he was guarded and wary, he soon expressed himself freely, articulating all kinds of resentments. Referring to his teachers, he said: "They tell me 'DO THIS—DO THAT—SIT DOWN.' They not fair, they don't like me."

In relation to the children, he would say: "They bother me. Linette sticks out her tongue and says, 'I'll tell my mother on you.'"

He wistfully communicated loneliness: "I have no friends."

Terry and Duane were both difficult, volatile children, but Terry's readiness for and responsiveness to help facilitated his growth.

Terry: (assembling the train set) I feel mad at my mother, she won't let my father come see me, she closes the door.
Teacher–Therapist: Some grownups don't get along.
Terry: Grownups are supposed to be nice and sweet. I get along with my mommy. See my eyes? They get mad (Terry could make his eyes blaze).
Teacher–Therapist: When you feel mad inside, you can make your eyes show it.

Another session showed Terry dealing with fury. He looked ready to explode. This was evident in his restless, undirected, random movements. The teacher–therapist tried to explore his feelings with him, but he shied away from her. She remarked that he looked as if he had a lot of strong feelings inside him, and that he had expressed this by throwing the doll puppet over.

Terry: I'm angry.
Teacher–Therapist: Would you like to throw darts? Sometimes that helps let off steam if someone feels ready to burst or is very angry.
Terry: I'm nervous in me.

He had a workout with the darts showing he could "hit" the numbers. He responded to naming the numbers and did it correctly. Suddenly he noticed Linette watching; with a menacing look on his face, he got two heavy, wooden mallets and said to her, "You're not coming here." Linette, realistically scared, jumped into the teacher–therapist's arms. Terry's eyes were blazing, his expression angry, and his manner threatening. The teacher–therapist assured Linette that she would not let Terry hit her; he was only telling her that he wanted to play alone. The teacher–therapist said to Terry, "Put down the mallets. You play here; Linette can play at the table."

Linette was relieved and accepted this idea easily, seeming to understand the explanation that "Terry was having a hard time today and he felt angry with everyone."

Terry stalked over and said, "I'm so strong and angry," demonstrating his anger by throwing the children's clothes out of their cubbies onto the floor.

Teacher–Therapist: You are angry. I can tell you're angry by your voice and eyes. What made you so angry?
Terry: Linette, she always tells me she's going to tell my mother and she tells me to shut up and that big fat lady (referring to one of the teachers), I punch her.

Teacher–Therapist: It makes you angry when Linette sticks out her tongue because you told me you want her to be your friend.

Terry climbed up onto his teacher–therapist's lap, relaxed, and allowed himself to be cuddled. He suddenly got up and walked to Linette.

Teacher–Therapist: You like to see what Linette is making.
Terry: Yes.
Teacher–Therapist: Do you feel better now?
Terry: I play with Linette.

Linette graciously showed Terry what she was doing.

Teacher–Therapist: Terry is over being angry and he wants to play with you now.
Linette: We'll make a party.

Terry said he would fix the juice; the rest of the time the two children played together setting up the "party table." In each instance in which a conflict arose, Terry controlled himself and listened to Linette. The children then played house; Terry was the husband, Linette the sister and wife. The play held together. Terry was able to control himself; he did not flick the lights on and off, even when Linette egged him on. The teacher–therapist reiterated, "Terry was angry and got over it. Linette was scared and got over being scared and the two are having fun . . . a happy time."

At the end of the session, Linette picked the story. The children listened and only at the end did Terry protest, wanting to have the book. This was prevented when the teacher–therapist held him saying, "Let's ask Linette if you can have her turn."

Linette: No, it my turn.
Teacher–Therapist: Linette said no but you can look in
    a minute.

There was a burst of anger as Terry kicked at a chair but Linette was able to have her turn.

Teacher–Therapist: Terry is going to have his turn but you
    don't have to wait. You can go to your room yourself
    or I'll take you.
Linette: Go myself.
Teacher–Therapist: Just like you go for the juice yourself.

Linette beamed as she left the room. (She was encouraged to leave so she would not experience Terry's anger again, since leaving the playroom often precipitated a great deal of conflict.)

Terry looked at the pictures in the book and then insisted on taking a policeman's badge with him. Since toys usually stay in the playroom, he accepted having the badge put into a box with his name on it, and left it in a special spot in the playroom. He then raced out of the room, down the hall, and sat in a cubby outside his nursery room, refusing to go into the room.

The teacher–therapist said she would wait for him in the nursery room and he could come in when he was ready; his regular nursery teacher would be glad to see him. He came into the room after twenty seconds, greeting his teacher in a friendly way.

In the following session, highly emotional material, very

similar to Duane's, was aired, but again Terry used the tools to help him cope much more effectively than Duane.

Terry was greeted with "How are you?"

Terry: I'm fine.
Teacher–Therapist: I'm glad you're fine.
Terry: Why?
Teacher–Therapist: I like you to feel good.
Terry: (listening with a grave expression) I'm angry! My father broke the door down. I want to live with my father. I told my mother.

The teacher–therapist agreed it made him angry that he couldn't live with his father. When he described how he punched his mother, the teacher–therapist told him he could punch the punching bag when he was angry. It could be a mother or a father or the therapist—anyone he wanted it to be. Terry promptly went over and vigorously punched the punching bag. She told him that when he was angry at all the fighting at home and at not seeing his father, he could punch the bag as hard as he could; but when he was with his friends, they didn't know he was angry at something at home. Terry listened intently and then went to set up the train tracks. Terry trusted and responded to his teacher–therapist's concern and interest by revealing his resentments and worries. Duane resisted becoming trusting, and remained hostile, guarded, and wary, fencing verbally throughout the year.

Terry developed an amazing ability to sense the onslaught of his own uncontrollable rage. The teacher–therapist showed him he could contain and handle this anger when he stopped long enough to communicate the trouble and be assured he would be heard and sup-

ported. It was unusual for a five year old to respond in
such a direct way.

There were times when he could not tolerate the children intruding upon him:

Terry: (angrily yelling) I'm the boss. I tell what to do!
Teacher–Therapist: You're the boss of yourself, yes. But
    in here I take care of everyone and help you and help
    Linette, George, Judy, and Danny.
Terry: (kicking a chair) They get too near me.

He then gathered the cowboys and settled himself in
the back part of the room.

Terry: I won't let anyone bother me.
Teacher–Therapist: You feel you need to play by yourself
    now, and that's O.K. Later, you may want to play with
    the children.

He continued to use separation at times of stress. The
periods of self–isolation grew less frequent and his feelings
became friendlier towards the other children.

As his anger dissipated and he had less need to be
"big and tough," his social relationships became gratifying
and scenes like the following nearly disappeared.

Terry banged his head with his fist saying, "You know
what's wrong with me—some people don't like me. Who
cares? Nobody cares . . ."

As his violent rages lessened, he revealed his percep-
tiveness, saying to Danny, "Punch the bag, you'll feel better;" to the teacher–therapist, "I wish I could stay here
all day" (replacing the tantrums he usually had upon leaving); to Linette, when she was screaming, "You can have

the book next time;" and again to Linette, "Why are you so scared all the time?"

The change carried over into his regular nursery group. He became more relaxed and a full participant in all activities. He built complicated and well–designed structures, enjoying his competency. Aggressive encounters with the other children became appropriate to the normal give and take of play. There were occasional expressions of tenderness, and a willingness to share candy and toys brought from home.

By the end of the year, although Terry was still triggered into anger, he could now control himself and recover quickly from a mood. He had made progress. He is still a vulnerable child but not so easily overwhelmed, and is able to function in a normal school setting. He has had to adjust to his mother's remarriage and the finality of not having his own father in the house. At the time of this writing, Terry is in third grade. Apart from being tutored in arithmetic, his level of scholastic performance is average to good. He seems more at ease with his world and has not presented any behavioral problem.

Juan

Juan's teacher described him as a child "who takes whatever he wants; his first reaction is to slug and hit out. He's angry, very aggressive, and he listens to no one."

The teacher–therapist saw a very handsome, intense, Spanish child; the sadness in his brown eyes struck her immediately. He was sturdy and well–built, but moved in a stodgy, slow–paced way. By not participating, he kept himself isolated in a group situation. There was an intensity about him, a noticeable lack of spontaneity, and a guarded quality. The negativism his teacher spoke of was very apparent. He pursued his own activities, not wanting to join the group for juice, toileting, or any of the daily routines. He shut out any request that impinged on his wishes by closing his eyes. He refused to move away from the paints, answer the teacher, or react to an adult. However, with a peer it was a different matter. For instance, when a child momentarily blocked his vision, his first response was a jump to anger. Striking out verbally or physically, he yelled, "Get out of here, you stupid fucker," pushing a child out of his way, kicking or grabbing a toy that was being used with no regard for or awareness of the other child. He appeared very unhappy in his loneliness and anger.

The psychiatrist found a very depressed, negative, little boy. He was sullen and unresponsive, but the tough façade covered a vulnerable, frightened, and pathetic child who reacted out of fear. He felt no one liked him, not his mother or his father—and he had no friends. He was an aggressive loner, actually suffering from feelings of inadequacy, loss of love, and lowered self–esteem. He felt unworthy of love, and needed to be accepted and nurtured. The teacher–therapist's role would be to present him with a different image of himself.

The psychologist's report indicated that Juan had a very shaky self–concept, and that he felt he lived in a dog–eat–dog world. He used avoidance as a defense against being put on the spot, his concentration wavered, and he was overwhelmed by strong emotions.

His intellectual functioning was disturbed. He had very poor language development, and had scored 88 on the Stanford–Binet Intelligence Scale.

The mothering he had received was very inconsistent, and he was overwhelmed by his mother's irrational controls. At one moment she would explode into anger and beat him with a strap or stick in an attempt to control him; at other times, she would bribe him with candy and toys. She frequently told him she would leave him, using this potential loss as a constant threat.

When Juan came to see the TNG room for the first time, he walked silently by the side of the teacher–therapist who felt very sure of his readiness to respond in the small group. He looked around the room, walked to the toy shelf, patted the woolly animals, and splashed his hand in the water as he passed the water table. Then he questioned:

Juan: I come here?
Teacher–Therapist: Yes.
Juan: (with a shy smile) I like it.
Teacher–Therapist: I'm glad you like it. When you come tomorrow, Thomas, Dick, Maria, and Laurie will come with you.

In a flash, the openness was gone; he was a sullen, little boy who had withdrawn into himself again.

Teacher–Therapist: I'll still be able to see what you like and listen to you. Even though the other children will be here, I'll be able to see what you like to play with.
Juan: O.K.

At the first session, the teacher–therapist collected the TNG children from the playground. Juan spotted her approaching and jumped off the bicycle he was riding. Racing over to her, he bumped into Thomas who was also coming towards her. The teacher–therapist remarked: "You're a fast runner, like a racer." Juan beamed. The teacher–therapist did not mention his bumping into Thomas, since Thomas had not reacted, and since Juan's bumping into a child or knocking over an object was the usual focus of an adult response to him. Juan's agility and coordination was brought to his attention by this realistic praise, long overdue for a child who was totally confined within a negative self–image. His aggressive behavior generally made it difficult for one to respond to him in a positive way, but the teacher–therapist was paving the way for future work with Juan by immediately recognizing and stressing that he did do certain things well.

Most of Juan's interaction in the TNG room was with two boys, Thomas and Dick, whose cases are not treated fully here. It is worth noting, however, that Thomas—a borderline child who suffered from a neurological disturbance resulting in frenzied tantrums—was extremely possessive about equipment, constantly battled with other children, and badly needed firm external controls. Similarly, Dick had very low frustration tolerance, but he generally hid his rage behind an ingratiating smile and calm manner.

In the first session, although he was constantly on the verge of explosive behavior which the teacher–therapist kept averting, Juan managed to maintain control of himself. At juice time he grabbed a package of Saltines that was still wrapped up. He started to rip the paper off.

Thomas: You don't know how.
Teacher–Therapist: There are two packages—one for each of you to open, and then there will be enough crackers for all of us.

The other three children watched the two boys.

Thomas: Here, I got it.
Juan: You tear it.

With delight, the two boys ripped open the packages and then Thomas, imitating Juan, started throwing the crackers on the floor. The boys ignored the basket for the crackers but did put them in when the teacher–therapist said, "They go in here."

Thomas and Juan left the juice table and went over to the darts. As Thomas hit the bull's eye, he said, "I'm the winner." Juan hit one of the numbers, kicked Thomas, and exclaimed, "I'm big, Thomas, I'm big!" The teacher–therapist gently led Juan away from Thomas and commented that both boys had done remarkably well by hitting the target. This comment enabled the play to continue for a brief period, but the competitive theme of big, bigger, better, best continued as they played together. Thomas went over to the woolly animals saying, "I'm taking care of this tiger." Juan tried to hand him a smaller tiger—which Thomas would not accept—saying, "Make believe my tiger is stronger than your tiger." Juan's tiger pawed at Thomas' tiger, as Thomas said, "The big tiger's gonna kill the little tiger." But instead of getting more involved, Thomas started to build. "Have to make a zoo."

Juan started his own building next to Thomas who got up and gathered all the animals, clutching them possessively.

Juan: He's not giving me any!
Teacher–Therapist: Thomas feels like having them all now for his zoo; you have your tiger.

Juan accepted this and continued to build a very simple structure, indifferent to his tiger lying next to him. In their regular nursery room, the two boys had great difficulty playing near each other, so this sustained contact, even though it had an explosive quality, was most unusual.

In the next session, although Dick, Juan, and Thomas had selected what they wanted to play with, they finally did not use any of the materials. Instead, they engaged in a constant battle over equipment, each wanting what the other had. The teacher–therapist would intervene, holding the toy they were fighting over. "Juan wants what Thomas has, Thomas wants what Juan has. Both boys want the same thing. What can you do about it?" Juan kicked Thomas; Thomas retaliated, and then was visibly upset—perhaps by his own aggression.

Teacher–Therapist: That makes a fight. Let's find another
    way so you two can play together as you started to.
Juan: Darts! I'm sorry.
Thomas: My mother says not to say you're sorry because
    I'm not sorry.
Teacher–Therapist: But Juan said he *was* sorry. Darts are
    a good idea, a good way to figure it out. There are
    enough for everyone.

By saying he was sorry, Juan indicated he was aware of Thomas' reaction. This awareness was used to help him develop peer relationships.

By session five, Juan was running to greet the teacher–therapist. At this session there were no battles. Juan was engrossed in the xylophone all session. He seemed comfortable with himself, singing a pumpkin song. (He had received a candy pumpkin from the teacher–therapist for Halloween.)

By late October, Juan began reacting to routines in the play room with much more acceptance. But several weeks

later, as the teacher–therapist arrived on the playground
to pick up the boys, they were fighting over a ball. Juan
was kicking Thomas and Thomas was kicking and pulling
Juan. The teacher–therapist stepped between them asking,
"What's the matter?" Juan started to explain, and Thomas
protested Juan's telling. The teacher–therapist said,
"Thomas, you'll have a turn to tell me too." The essence
of the intervention is often not to judge, not to condemn,
just to listen; each child feels his view is important. With
encouragement, Juan told his story, then listened, scowling,
as Thomas told his story. Juan dropped the ball and ran
ahead to the playroom.

This competitiveness continued in the session. Thomas
and Juan started building. Dick was working with the
trains, grumbling when he couldn't connect them
immediately. He tried to involve himself with Juan and
Thomas in a bossy but half–hearted way. (An earlier effort
by the teacher–therapist to include Dick in their play had
been unsuccessful.) Thomas cried bitterly over a fire engine
and spat at Juan who tried to take it from him. Juan spat
back saying, "You spit—I spit." Thomas then picked up
a block and was aiming it at Juan. The teacher–therapist
took the block from Thomas, who then zipped over, filled
a cup with water, and tossed it toward Juan. Juan looked
stunned. Thomas became very upset—probably fearful of
his own rage and Juan's retaliation. It took the rest of the
session to quiet Thomas down. While the teacher–therapist
held Thomas on her lap, Juan joined Dick and helped him
connect the train tracks. (Previously Juan had walked over
Dick's tracks, sending them spinning across the room. At
that time Dick had merely shrugged his shoulders in
response to the teacher–therapist's, "Does that bother you,
Dick?"). Thomas was calm enough at the end of the session
to select the story to be read.

Teacher–Therapist: (to Thomas as he picked a book) You were able to calm yourself down.

Thomas: I was very upset. (He has a precocious ability to verbalize his feelings.)

Juan finished putting the last two tracks in place and then joined the group for the story, sitting next to Thomas. His ability to function with another child, even for a brief time, indicated he was beginning to relate.

In November, the teacher–therapist met Juan and his mother entering the nursery school. Mrs. T. said, "Juan say, 'Mary Jane bueno.'" Juan looked at the teacher–therapist and nodded his head. As she walked with them to his regular classroom, the teacher–therapist told Juan she would pick him up later. When she returned, Juan smiled in response to her greeting, and suddenly climbed into her lap, while she waited for the other three children to get ready. As he left the nursery room he called to the children, "Goodbye." Several children yelled, "Goodbye, Juan." Juan stood still, blinking his eyes; he looked overwhelmed by their response. Juan was unusually calm during the TNG session. Thomas was absent, which probably helped Juan maintain his control.

At juice time, Juan gave an accurate rendition of how Gregory had broken his plastic plane. Dick kept interrupting; Juan did not fly into anger, but said, in an exasperated tone, "I'm telling." This ability to verbalize instead of hitting was reinforced by the teacher–therapist who said, "You are telling." Dick then chose to play with the trains. Juan stood silently near him. Soon the two boys were playing together, assembling the tracks. Dick kept telling Juan what to do.

Teacher–Therapist: (to Dick) You tell Juan what to do, but then you don't let him.

Dick: (impatiently and angrily) I'll let him! I'll let him.
But you cut out the pumpkin mask. (As the
teacher–therapist continued cutting out the pumpkin
mask with Maria and Laurie) Did you do the nose?
Why didn't you? Why don't you do the mouth? Not
there—cut it there.

Teacher–Therapist: You're telling Juan and me, "Do this,
do that, do it this way, do it that way." No right way
for you today?

Dick didn't answer. He walked over and looked at the
Halloween mask.

Teacher–Therapist: Did you wear a mask at Halloween?
Dick: (in a complaining voice) I couldn't get out. My mother
wouldn't let me.
Teacher–Therapist: Oh, maybe that's why today you think
nobody does anything right.

She handed the mask to Dick, who smiled and put it
on. Laurie and Marie sang a song about the pumpkin. Dick
returned to play with Juan, who had been listening intently
to the conversation. Juan suddenly used the train to demonstrate how his father had tried to get into a parking space.
Dick laughed at the accurate mimicry.

At the end of the session, the teacher–therapist was
able to reiterate the positive aspects of the session. "Dick
had felt grumpy, but then he began to feel happier. Juan
listened all morning, and when he goes back to the classroom he can listen and then he'll have a happier time."
It was necessary to link Juan's behavior in TNG with the
regular nursery room and to try in this way to ease the
tension he created in the classroom.

Juan: (understanding and translating into concrete terms
his attempt to follow his classroom routines) And when
it's time to go to lunch, I go to lunch.

This comment illustrated the beginning of Juan's understanding of and awareness of his own behavior.

There was noticeable carry–over into the next TNG session. Dick was in a pleasant mood, saying to Juan, "Will
you build with me?" Juan replied, "You bet!" and they
enthusiastically built a tunnel. The fun seemed to be in
putting the train through the tunnel and watching it come
out the other side. Juan figured out a ramp system so the
train had enough momentum to carry it all the way through
the tunnel. Dick accepted Juan's idea and after a few
minutes turned to the teacher–therapist.

Dick: It's a beautiful day.
Teacher–Therapist: It is. How do you feel about a beautiful
day?
Dick: Good. (To Juan, in a gruff, pseudo–bossy tone) Juan,
you know what to do. Fix it.
Juan: (smiling, pleased at Dick's compliment) Come on,
you help me too.

When Dick screamed and grumbled later in the session
because he couldn't connect a track, Juan became the
therapeutic agent.

Juan: Why you scream like that? You scream like a baby.

Dick looked stunned. Marie and Laurie, who were
building nearby, laughed. Juan then smiled at Dick; Dick
stopped screaming and smiled, too. The impact of the chil-

dren on each other was clearly helpful; the interaction with Dick was beneficial to Juan as well as to Dick.

During another session, Juan tried to take the fire engine from Laurie, who insistzd that he couldn't have it. She teasingly handed it to Dick, instead. Juan looked at the teacher–therapist:

Teacher–Therapist: Laurie, do you want it?
Laurie: No.
Teacher–Therapist: Juan didn't ask you. Is that the trouble?
Laurie: Yes. (She then took the fire engine from Dick and handed it to Juan.)
Juan: Thanks. (A different Juan.)

Laurie was so surprised, she quickly handed Juan another fire engine. Maria and Laurie then began a jumping game on the steps; for the first time the boys spontaneously joined the girls for an activity. Juan was obviously interacting more freely with the other children.

The following session, when Thomas returned after having been ill, Juan was noticeably upset. He sat with the mini–dolls, stuffed them in the house, and shut them in. He had withdrawn into himself and did not respond to any attempt to engage him in activities. However, when Thomas socked Maria, who had accidentally broken a spoon, Juan hit and bit Thomas. Thomas was held on the teacher–therapist's lap until he calmed down.

Thomas: I'm strongest.
Juan: I'm strongest.
Teacher–Therapist: Both of you boys are strong. I think Juan feels if Thomas is here I won't be able to help him or Maria. But there's enough of me to help all the children.

At this juncture, Juan slowly began to accept having the same number of blocks as others and sharing not only the blocks, the fire engines, and the cars, but the teacher's attention as well. He began responding to limits such as "one more minute." The session structure was presented to him in such a way that he would have time for all he wanted to do—blocks, water, and planned activities—and be prepared for the difficulty of leaving the TNG room as well.

The psychiatrist observed him in the playroom at this time. She said that the sharing relationship he was developing was remarkable. The speed with which he had come to feel comfortable in the playroom did not bear out the intensity of disturbed behavior which had showed up on the psychological examination. And yet, in the regular nursery room there was no dramatic behavioral change. His play was still fragmentary. He became wild, disorganized, and overstimulated by the other children, and was difficult to manage.

At Christmas time, Thomas was also having a hard time, the playroom session was touch and go, although there was no real eruption. When Thomas was picked up in his regular nursery room for the session he was running about, banging a chair up and down.

Teacher–therapist: What's the matter, Thomas?
Thomas: I want to do what I want to do!

He looked pale, tired, and very tense, his fingers fluttering rapidly in obvious anxiety. Although he came willingly to the playroom, he cried at the slightest provocation. He seemed to like his Christmas gift but it did not hold his interest for more than a few moments.

At this session, Juan was delighted with his gift, but it did not help him over his restless, irritated mood. He looked sad and his attention span was limited. He could not tolerate frustration and when asked if something were bothering him, he said, "No," even though he was obviously upset.

Thomas and Juan could not sustain any play situation on this particular day. Juan felt rejected by Thomas, who several times refused to play with him. Neither boy became involved in anything. The teacher–therapist observed, "You and Juan are both upset today. Thomas said, 'I want to do what I want to do,' and Juan couldn't find anything he wants to do. Let's listen to records together (eliminating the need for them to interact)."

Holidays always seemed a difficult time for the children in the TNG groups. The overexcitement due to the talk about presents and the admonitions to "be good, or else," were added pressure.

However, after the holidays the boys continued to work out a relationship. Thomas had fallen off the slide and was crying bitterly. Juan sat on the ground next to him, patting him on the arm, trying to comfort him. This was the beginning of the emergence of Juan's strong capacity for empathy. During the session Thomas was in a dress–up navy suit. He and Juan marched around the room. Dick wanted to wear the suit. Juan told the teacher–therapist, "You should have three suits for three boys."

Another time Juan brought a rocket to school and was eager to show it off. Thomas was bursting to play with it and began impatiently teasing Juan.

Thomas: I'm not your friend. I'm not your friend.
Juan: I'm your friend; don't say you're not my friend. (This stopped Thomas.)
Teacher–Therapist: Friends can be friends even if he doesn't do what you always want him to do.

Then Juan let Thomas, as well as the other children, have a turn, after which the teacher–therapist put the rocket on the shelf.

Dick: When I don't do what my mother wants she's still my friend, even when she hits me. (Parroting the adult in a psuedo–mature way, his words had a hollow sound.)
Teacher–Therapist: That's true, but it does hurt to be hit. Mothers get angry and get over being angry just like friends.
Dick: Mothers feel bad when they hit you.

Juan said nothing, but his expression was intense and serious as he listened. Thomas went right back to teasing for the rocket, although he did have a turn. Juan lifted his hand to sock him, but then turned and punched the punching bag. Thomas laughed, delighted and relieved, and socked it too.

Teacher–Therapist: Juan, you were able to stop yourself.
Juan: (Socking the punching bag again) Say it again, Mary Jane.
Teacher–Therapist: You were able to stop yourself. (This supported and reinforced his growing ability to master his impulse to jump to anger.)

The session ended with Dick joining Juan and Thomas under the steps. Dick had taken the cracker basket and the boys were having a picnic party. Juan, eager to stay in the playroom, kept coming out to turn the hands of the clock back. The developing relationship between the three boys was seen more vividly at the next session when Juan was sick. Thomas's behavior was diffuse; he fussed and he couldn't settle down with anything.

Teacher–Therapist: You wanted Juan to be here today.

Thomas: He's my friend. (Thomas's basic problem was his fear of abandonment and this seemed reactivated by Juan's absence.)

There were still many angry outbursts among the children but they were becoming more manageable. The theme of working out relationships was the focus at this point. Not only did the teacher–therapist plan her interventions with this in mind, but the children themselves, through their identification with her, were also therapeutic agents.

Dick: (to Juan who had just taken his train) Juan, you just take, you don't ask.

Thomas: (picking up on this) Why do you take so much?

Teacher–Therapist: He's learning.

Juan: (not answering, but knocking part of Dick's building down) I didn't mean to! (He started to build it up with assistance from the teacher–therapist. Although he responded indirectly, he was obviously showing he understood what the teacher–therapist was saying. Then, to Thomas) Will you make a kite for me?

Thomas, boosted by Juan's request, first drew one kite and then an anchor. Then both boys worked on it together, pulling a string through the paper anchor. Juan's attempt to reinstate himself with both boys was an indicator of his growing friendships.

The theme carried over into the next session. Juan took the navy hat from Thomas's head. Thomas blasted Juan, calling him names and insulting him. "You act like a three year old." This triggered Juan's explosiveness. He tossed a boat at Thomas and then went after him. Thomas'

immediate reaction was to lunge at Juan. The teacher–
therapist held Juan on her lap to prevent a real physical
encounter, saying, "It makes Thomas angry when you take
his things." Thomas then repeated, "It makes me angry,
Juan." Then the teacher–therapist pointed out to Thomas,
"This time you could talk to Juan and Juan could understand." As Juan snuggled in her lap she added, "Juan's
learning about not taking; sometimes he remembers and
sometimes he forgets." Juan jumped off her lap and ran
over to the punching bag saying, "I punch Joe Palooka."
Apparently he remembered his successful displacement
of anger in a previous session. Thomas, more relaxed but
still wary of Juan, said, "You punch him." Juan then put
the navy hat back on and began to make a boat, using the
blocks.

Thomas's need to be separate from Juan was evident,
and Juan seemed to sense this because, instead of trying
to join Thomas, he selected the hammer and pegboard set.
He made the shape of a house and sat contentedly hammering as he put a roof on the house.

Teacher–Therapist: Anybody in your house?
Juan: People.

This was the first time he had ever included anyone else.
Juan selected his favorite story, *Curious George,* to be
read, and then took the cowboys and horses from the shelf
and enacted part of the story.

Juan: The monkey, he's bad. He locked in the bathroom.
    He hit.
Teacher–Therapist: The monkey was bad. What did he do?
Juan: Monkey jumped on the horse and runs away.

Teacher–Therapist: He felt badly about being locked in
the bathroom; it's hard for the little monkey to be good
all the time.
Juan: (pensively) Yeah.

(Juan was often very severely punished at home; he
identified with the naughty monkey. The teacher–
therapist was trying to help him feel understood.)

At the next session, Juan came into the playroom early
and helped set up the juice and crackers. The teacher–
therapist had waved to him from the window as he was
entering school. She asked him if he would like to play
in the yard until it was time for the group to come.

Juan: No. Play with you. (He waved goodbye to his mother
and said to her, in English) I stay with Mary Jane. (She
smiled pleasantly at him. His face was glowing with
pleasure at staying.)
Teacher–Therapist: You're happy today.

This kind of specific verbalization often helps the child
become aware of his feelings and their impact. Juan's good
mood continued through the session. He worked briefly
with Thomas, helping him build a tunnel for the trains,
and then used the cowboys when Thomas said he wanted
to play alone. Juan accepted the teacher–therapist's pointing out of reality, "Juan, you played with Thomas, now
you play with the cowboys; friends can be friends and
not do the same things." Juan repeated the whole statement, as if assimilating it.

Thomas now showed a growing ability to sense when
he needed to play alone, although there were many sessions
when he still had a diffuse quality. Thomas continued to
require immediate and constant support. During this par-

ticular session, he made a frogman's wings and pretended to swim. He whined, "I don't know how to get out," and then he seemed relieved when the teacher–therapist said, "Swim to the top." It was time to end the session and Thomas looked woebegone, unable to accept this fact.

Juan: (solicitously) Thomas, remember when you were happy?
Thomas: I'm NOT HAPPY.

Thomas became furious, tossed paper at Juan, and then became extremely fearful that Juan would retaliate. Juan did not do so until the group was leaving the room. Then he kicked Thomas, who dissolved in tears. As the teacher–therapist approached Thomas, he grabbed her glasses, pulled her necklace, and hit out. She held him on her lap and sent the other children ahead to their room. He suddenly relaxed, then seemed to collapse on her lap, saying, "I'm sick. I'm very sick." (Thomas was very perceptive; he was coming down with pneumonia. When children are physically sick, they are more vulnerable to the slightest stress and when controls, which are tenuous at best, are weakened, regression is the first clue to impending illness.) When Thomas returned to school the boys continued to interact.

Dick: I make Superman suit.
Juan: I can't make nothing like that.
Dick: I'll make it for you.

Dick worked on his own suit and on one for Juan, who helped by taping the pieces together.

Juan: Who's the bad Superman? Not me.

Dick: I'll be the bad Superman and we'll fight.

Dick started to chase Juan, who looked frightened and became over–excited. The teacher–therapist stopped the boys with, "It's an interesting game, but it gets you too excited; let's find something else to play." Both boys objected.

Dick: You don't have new toys; you don't have a TV so we can watch.
Juan: Your hair is silly.
Teacher–Therapist: It made you angry when I stopped your game.

Both boys shut her out, talking to each other.

Dick: I'm not scared by monsters on TV.
Juan: My sister watches them. I no like monsters.
Teacher–Therapist: Would you like to see some monster pictures I have?

The long–awaited opportunity to point out the make–believe quality of monsters and the use of costumes usually presents itself around Halloween. However, in this year of TNG, the children were not ready for it until the end of the year. As the teacher–therapist took out the pictures, the children dashed over to the table and sat down, looking very serious. Dick immediately identified Frankenstein.

Juan: I'm scared.
Dick: (pointing to one) That's the outer space monster. I get frightened.
Juan: You scared of this one, Dick?
Dick: No, he's almost like a man.

Juan: I want to look at this one (a man wrapped in bandages with only slits for his eyes, nose, and mouth).

He studied it. The teacher–therapist took a doll and bandages, demonstrating how the bandages could be wrapped round a man's face. Juan needed to bandage and unbandage the doll repeatedly to convince himself that what he had seen on TV was really make–believe. Putting on a mask and pretending to be a monster is every child's attempt to gain mastery of fearful situations, such as the dark, or imaginary monsters. This mastery occurs through make–believe and play. Frequently, disturbed children have difficulty in separating reality from fantasy and, therefore, suffer an inordinate amount of fear. Showing them the reality does not remove the fear entirely, but it does help to control the intensity of the fear.

Thomas, looking at the pictures, insisted that he had known all along that it was all make–believe. Then:

Thomas: Make believe I'm the daddy.
Juan: Yeah, you make believe I'm the dog.

However, the game never started. Thomas became annoyed because Juan wasn't following his directions.

Thomas: You stupid, Juan.
Juan: Hey, you're stupid if you call me stupid.
Thomas: Stupid, you are not stupid now.
Juan: We are friends.
Thomas: You are not my friend.
Juan: Okay, you are my friend. (Juan was not shaken by Thomas' statement.)

More imaginative play developed as Juan felt less con-

stricted and more accepted by his peers. He was moving
out into new directions and his interests were expanding.
He tied a string to a box, used an old wall switch, incorporated a pulley, and played elevator, having the box stop
at different levels (floors) so he could unload furniture.
The other children were entranced by the new game.

At another time, he and Thomas turned the steps into
a boat. Juan pretended to dock the boat by tying it to a
hook on the wall. He then made a paper fish. Thomas
imitated him, then both boys pretended to go fishing.

The following session's tempo was extremely uneven.
The children again set up the steps as a boat. Their voices
were shrill and high; their tenseness created conflicts at
first. The teacher–therapist had to intervene a great deal
and the content of Thomas' play was aggressive, competitive, and conflictive. The teacher–therapist reminded them
of the good time they had had in the previous session.
This enabled them to diffuse and the tone of the play
changed, became more relaxed, and enabled them to
interact.

Thomas: There's Indians around our ship and they're going
    around.
Juan: Let's do something.
Thomas: Let's shout. (Then, in response to the shouts)
    Know what that is? Flying saucers.

Juan and Thomas made driving noises.

Thomas: This can be a motorboat.
Juan: Hey, I'm going to tie it up over here. There, Thomas,
    so the ship won't go away.
Thomas: Hey, let's go.
Dick: Can I play?

Teacher–Therapist: Ask them, Dick.

Juan and Thomas: (before he can ask) Get out of here!

Teacher–Therapist: (supporting Dick) Here comes another sailor.

Dick: (not sure) Can I play?

Juan: Yeah, but you need a hat.

Thomas: (from the back of the room) Don't let Dick play.

Thomas accepted the teacher–therapist's reassurance that he would still have fun even if Dick was the third sailor. Juan and Thomas decided which hat Dick would wear and finally chose a jungle hat, still bossing Dick, who didn't protest.

Dick: (to teacher–therapist) Is this right? It bothers me. (The teacher–therapist fixes it for him.)

Thomas: Those boxes, those are boxes that we put our treasure in. (Juan and Thomas swagger back to get more boxes.) Take the basket also. Put it on the ship decks. Put 'em in the garage. This can be the garage too.

Juan: No, this one.

Thomas: Please, this can be the garage (He was very tense and said this urgently.) Put 'em in this one too. We have to sit in the captain part. Now we have to untie the ship. (He gets off.)

Dick: Wait, we forgot something. We forgot our bombs. Go and get them.

Thomas: Wait, I'll be back in a minute. Don't unloose the ship. We can keep the bombs here. We don't need the box.

Dick: Hurry up. Ship's about to leave.

Thomas: C'mon, let's swim. The boat is sinking. Let's get in front.

At this point the play became too real. Thomas ran into

the closet, isolating himself from the other children.

Teacher–Therapist: Here comes another boat to help the
sailors.

Thomas jumped on the new boat and the game continued until table time.

The imaginative play and his growing ability to participate in a group was real progress for Juan. Thomas had
been important for Juan's growth—he was his first friend.
This first year ended with considerable gains for Juan and
the summary report indicated the year's progress.

Juan developed self–esteem and showed great improvement in socialization. His behavior changed in all areas
of functioning. He responded from the beginning to being
in the small group. Throughout many sessions Juan was
an angry boy. He had no tools for contact with the other
children. If he wanted, he took; if frustrated by them, he'd
hit or kick. His negativism showed in the way he literally
shut out requests and resisted routines. He had almost no
awareness of his own capabilities; and his play with materials was devoid of content. He responded almost immediately to praise and recognition. Juan had many qualities
which could be realistically praised, especially his later
accomplishments—development of self–control, less impulsive hitting and taking, and his growing compassion
for another child. During this year Juan began to experience
his assertiveness without fear of retaliation by an adult
figure.

At the end of the year, Juan was still extremely vulnerable, still covering up by acting tough. He could not tolerate
verbal taunting from the other children but was quite good
at retaliating. Juan began to initiate contacts with the other
children, particularly Thomas. In the beginning, he needed

a great deal of help sustaining his play as conflicts, which usually ended in a physical fight, developed. Gradually, as Juan began to feel better about himself, there were fewer angry outbursts. He frequently transferred his punches to the punching bag or into verbal attacks. His nursery school teacher reported that he was fighting less in the large group.

Juan indicated a capacity for warmth and responded to efforts to establish a relationship with him. He became quite verbal, describing in happy tones pleasurable times with his mother. Gradually he included his father in his conversations. One particular incident he described was his father playing cards and joking with a guest. He began to show the beginnings of a sense of humor. His eyes would sparkle when he sensed fun in a situation. He also began to enjoy the sound of words.

Juan's tempo was still fast, and his vitality and energy could often be overstimulating and develop into wild play. He needed help in harnessing and channeling this energy constructively. He had found it impossible to accept limits. However, although he still had difficulty in this area, he had improved. Initially, by pursuing his own interests, he had ignored any routines and requests imposed by the teacher–therapist. When he found that the limits were the same for each child in the group, he could accept them for himself, as he could respond to fairness. A great deal of Juan's hitting and taking seemed to taper off when he realized that there was enough of most things to go around.

However, certain situations were still very difficult for Juan to cope with. The fact that TNG sessions come to an end disturbed him and, at this point, he often ran and hid, becoming hostile, and defiant. The more trying sessions seemed to be related to his state of mind when he came to school in the morning. He often arrived looking angry or depressed, having suffered some form of punishment at home, and this irritation increased during the day. He spoke frequently of his fear of monsters and sought reassurance about their unreality.

The report at the end of the TNG year concluded that Juan was beginning to receive satisfaction from his relationships and his use of materials. Another year in TNG was recommended to help him consolidate his gains and hopefully, to work through his angry feelings so he could cope with them more effectively. We also felt it was imperative that Juan's mother receive some help in handling him.

The retesting of Juan emphasized the beneficial effects of his first TNG year. The psychologist found it significant that his I.Q. score of 98–102 was some ten or more points higher than in the previous test situation. Furthermore, his responses on the intelligence test displayed a distinct improvement not only in score, but also in the quality of his successes and failures. For example, on both tests he failed to put together two pieces of paper to form a rectangle. On previous testing, he had been totaly unable to do it by himself; at the second testing, though still incapable of doing the task alone, he was able to do it after being shown how. This reflected a change in attitude towards cooperation with authority figures. In this second session, he was much more willing to listen, take directions, and follow through with the task.

There was also greater clarity of thinking—a more direct, task–oriented quality—and there were fewer intrusions of emotionally charged thoughts when he tried to concentrate. For instance, when asked in his first testing why we have houses, he said, "Because we want to. Have no house, rain comes in to us and we get dead." At the later testing session he said, "Because we don't want to get wet." His greater clarity was also reflected in his ability to think through a problem that was not totally unfamiliar to him.

Thus, when asked for the difference between a bird and a dog the first time, he said, "I don't know," while the second time he said, "Dog got legs and bird got little, tiny legs and bird get wings and dog can't get it . . . but don't supposed to have wings."

He definitely showed an ability to abstract, although in some areas he remained shaky. Number concepts and vocabulary were still poor and needed work. His visual motor coordination, though better, left much to be desired.

The tests in general revealed a decided improvement in Juan's ability to gain control over strong feelings of which he was afraid, yet which pushed for expression. There was still a volcanic sense about him, but the urgency for and tenuousness of defenses seen previously had decreased. Even though he remained anxious and still experienced a sense of danger and of being overwhelmed, he seemed to have greater ego strength—a bit more assurance that he would not crumble. Because of this, he could relate better to others. His fantasies were not so aggressively tainted, and the need for bravado that was so much a part of him was diminished.

Nevertheless, with this improvement he could not maintain a relatively trouble–free existence consistently. The roots of his anger seemed untouched and the ferocity of its push for expression was still there, although slightly lessened. He certainly needed more help.

In September, Juan's nursery school teacher reported that he was having an extremely difficult time again. His mood had changed dramatically. He looked very sad and he was tuning out his friends as well as adults. She described finding him standing outside the playroom, crying and asking for the teacher–therapist.

The social worker reported that Juan's mother had become very depressed, cried a great deal, and felt unable to cope with her husband, and that Juan was being used as a pawn in their battles.

During the preliminary formulation of the new TNG group, Juan was seen immediately and individually because of his crisis. (The other children from the previous year had moved away, or gone on into first grade.) The teacher–therapist found he had turned inward, looked depressed, and responded in a mechanical fashion. He needed a great deal of reassurance. Juan kept repeating, in a tone of great intensity, "I stay, I stay." His relationship with the teacher–therapist had to be re-established since it was difficult for him to bridge the separation over the summer. Apparently, his mother had become less available to him during the same period.

The teacher–therapist spoke with Juan's mother about his summer. She looked sad and said, "Juan talks in his sleep. He say, 'Mary Jane.' He wants you and doesn't like me." (Some parents experience resentment because of the close relationship their child develops with another person.) The teacher–therapist responded by assuring her that Juan also spoke of his mother to her and that some children use this device when they get angry. The teacher–therapist pointed out that Juan did this especially when he was being disciplined. Juan's mother then spoke of the difficulty she had in walking him to school, and that the only way she could control him was to carry a switch (a long branch). Appointments were set up with the social worker to try to help her with Juan, but she never kept them. As the year progressed, the family situation continued to deteriorate.

It took a number of sessions before Juan's heavy mood lifted, and then it was only for short periods. His depression as well as his strong feelings of anger were very apparent.

When the group sessions began in early October, he was still seen alone for five or ten minutes preceding each session. He found it very difficult to accept the new group, and spoke of how he missed Thomas.

One of the new children, Torro, triggered Juan into broiling fights. Because there was spontaneous combustion when the two boys attempted to play together, sustained play was impossible at first, although at times Juan made an effort to compromise. In spite of erupting with Torro, he was able to act as "host" to the two girls. He showed them all the toys in the room, especially the doll corner, and turned on the faucet for them so they could have a drink. The room was his "turf" and he really demonstrated that he felt comfortable about it.

By November, Juan seemed better and could become involved in figuring out things. He spent one entire session working with a Tinker Toy set to make a truck, talking as he worked. "When I grow up I be a policeman. Policemen let children do what they want. I told my father." (Juan wants to be in control.) Another time he made a pirate hat. He talked as he punched holes for string so he could wear it. As he put the hat on, it ripped; Juan nonchalantly said, "You can't win them all," laughed, and easily accepted some staples to remake the hat.

Although his frustration tolerance toward materials had greatly improved and he was now able to make connections between events, he was still as explosive as a dynamite keg. He had grown and become very sturdy, so that his anger lashed out with real force. For example, on one occasion, Torro couldn't stand Juan not playing with him and kicked at Juan's building without actually touching it. Juan then kicked Torro's building down with such force that the blocks went flying and hit Torro. Torro, outraged, flew into a tantrum, kicking and tossing equipment. The teacher–therapist calmed both boys, interpreting the chain of events, pointing out that Torro had wanted to play with Juan. Suddenly, Torro put his arm around Juan and they came to the table for a game. Torro generally did want to play with Juan, but their inflammability made it difficult for both.

Another incident demonstrated their volcanic relationship. Juan had offered Torro a rubber motorcycle, but Torro grabbed Juan's motorcycle instead. Juan started to kick him and stomp on his back. As the teacher–therapist stopped him, she removed his shoes. Juan stopped kicking and began to knock things off the shelf. He did calm down as she held him saying, "Five year olds don't have to kick. I know it makes you very mad when I take your shoes, but I can't let you kick Torro or me." Juan's pride had been hurt when his shoes were removed. Children strongly resent this kind of interference, feeling it is a real invasion of their being, but it was done out of the urgency of the moment. The teacher–therapist's tone was cross, and her own feelings of anger had been triggered when Juan stomped on Torro. But after the incident, Torro still continued to try to initiate play with Juan. Torro could only feel complete with another child or an adult. Juan could not tolerate his clinging. Because of the destructive interaction of the two boys, Juan was again seen alone, rather than in the group situation. It became evident that Juan would benefit more from being seen individually and the group would be more helpful to Torro.

Juan felt the change in plans as a punishment and a rejection. He sat silently, large tears running down his face, as the teacher–therapist explained he would have a time for himself and he could talk about the things he wanted to, or listen to a story, or use the toys. He remained unhappy, but by the end of the first individual session, he began to repeat, "It's a time just for me," and he seemed to accept and be more comfortable with the change.

In these individual sessions Juan began to reveal more of himself. He mentioned bad dreams. "I dream monsters, they have batteries in them, they come and get me. When I close my eyes I have lights so I can see." However, a little later he said, "Monsters are fake; it's a show." This was after he and his teacher–therapist talked about "the way they dress people up to look like monsters," recapitulating the sessions spent on this matter the previous year.

His being seen alone helped him to function a little better in the large room. He could stay involved with materials for long periods of time, which made him more maintainable, but was also indicative of a drawing inward. There were, however, instances where he spontaneously shared a toy, and most important, the children were no longer afraid of him.

In the individual sessions he began to express and share painful things. One day, he burst into the room, then sat in a chair at the table with a sad, forlorn expression. His eyelids were heavy. As the teacher–therapist went to close the door, Juan followed her and sat down on the floor, resting his back against a cubby. The teacher–therapist sat next to him.

Juan: I no like my name. It ugly.
Teacher–Therapist: What name do you like?
Juan: (mentioning a Spanish name) He my cousin.
Teacher–Therapist: Sometimes children don't like their names when they don't feel happy, or someone makes

them feel they are not nice. But children are really good and nice, even if they do naughty things sometimes. I know you are a very nice boy.

Juan: My father not nice, he threw my mother out of the car and she sat on the bench and cried.

Teacher–Therapist: I know that must have made you feel real sad inside, because you love your mother. It was a grown–up fight and it's so hard for a child to understand grown–up fights.

Juan nodded his head and leaned on her.

Teacher–Therapist: I've noticed that sometimes when you feel sad you act real tough and fight in school so no one knows how sad you feel.

Juan climbed into her lap. He looked so pathetically serious and his hurt was so apparent that she put her arms around him saying, "I know you are feeling sad, but I'm glad you can talk about it, and I'm glad you told me."

The year was drawing to a close and in the last few sessions the many things he had learned to do were reiterated. He was the fastest runner in the school; he could build beautiful buildings; he had some friends; and now he could talk about what made him feel sad and did not need to act so tough. His mood continued to be sad. The ending of the group was probably a contributing factor, but more central was the home situation.

Juan was certainly feeling more competent in relation to skills and he coped with his violent feelings by withdrawing. He had certainly established a trusting relationship with the teacher–therapist and made gains in socialization.

However, his perceptual difficulties resulted in fearfulness in attempting to draw or engage in any activity he felt he could not master. He needed much help in overcoming these fears. The psychiatrist still felt, "His inner world is violent and he is in danger of exploding with uncontrollable force. He must learn to control the impulses."

His mother was seen at the end of the year in order to set up psychiatric treatment for Juan since he was moving into first grade. She seemed very pleased and proudly talked of all that Juan was learning. She also reported that Juan was more attentive now and had said to her, "You don't have to tell me two times." She mentioned that Juan had gone into a trance while watching TV and she had to slap him to bring him out of it.

Although tentative plans were again made for Juan to get psychiatric help in his first school year, the family disappeared and could not be located.

The limitations of the TNG program were strikingly apparent in Juan's case. His family could not be reached on any long-term or constructive fashion and its disintegration was playing havoc with Juan. Although attempts were made to get individual psychiatric treatment for him, and to involve the mother with counselling service, none of these plans materialized.

Even though the TNG program was not able to fully solve Juan's personal and familial difficulties, it did constitute a situation in which, perhaps for the first time, he could feel himself being listened to, loved, and accepted. The support of the teacher–therapist, as well as of other children in the group, established the basis for a positive sense of himself which would hopefully sustain him in the many moments of pain he would undoubtedly encounter.

Follow-up Contact with Schools

Virtually all of the TNG children who reach school age attend a neighborhood public or parochial school. The Hudson Guild and the Counseling Service, in particular, maintain a close working relationship with these schools to get further feedback on the progress of the TNG children. In addition, we attempt to place the youngsters in a relatively benign atmosphere by holding conferences with teachers and school guidance counselors on those children who are likely to find the transition and adjustment to elementary school difficult. By discussing the child's problems, we try to promote understanding and an individualized approach to the child in school. When the child has difficulty adjusting, the Counseling Service provides additional therapeutic help. Thus we maintain responsibility for and communication with the child after the termination of the TNG sessions.

Chapter 5

Summary

IN ANY DAY CARE CENTER or nursery school, teachers can pick out the children who need some special help. (Thirty percent of the children studied in six day care centers needed help [Kohn, 1969]). At four and five these children's difficulties already interfere with their ability to function in their society. We accept the hypothesis that it is perhaps the availability of an adequate mothering person in the first three years of a child's life that determines his ability to function. The child with fundamentally healthy mothering can cope with the diluted relationship he finds in nursery school; the others cannot. Whether the mothering is unavailable because of the pressures of inadequate housing, economic deprivation, or the degradation of welfare is a question of etiology. There are other children, however,

145

with similar difficult, even desperate, backgrounds who come in with the emotional equipment which enables them to function and remain on the developmental track.

Our experience has been that difficulties, even harrowing environmental circumstances, are not the key to the problems experienced by the children. Recent work in the Harvard Preschool Project revealed that whatever factors produced differences in the social and intellectual skills of two groups of children happened well before the age of three. Unless there is skilled intervention for the troubled child at an early age, the chance of such a child "making it" in any way is meager.

The relevance of intervention at an early age is obvious. The child of four or five is open to change, since his difficulties have not yet become an entrenched part of him. With skilled intervention, he can enter the public school system with at least a moderate chance of success.

Although these children might be referred to psychiatric clinics, the working or the overburdened mother is unlikely to follow through on psychiatric clinic referrals. Furthermore, clinics are not really prepared to meet the needs of the preschool child, and their waiting lists are often incredibly long. Ideally, one would hope to make help available within the day care center itself, as we have illustrated. First of all, here the child is available to the clinician on a regular basis, even when his family is not.

When involvement with the family is necessary, various alternate approaches are available. For example, contact with the parent can be made when the child is brought to school or picked up at the end of the day; in home visits; through community friends, etc. The day care center's location in the community lends itself to flexible and imaginative alternatives without the family having to deal with the fears, apprehension, and time involved in going to a clinic.

Most professionals feel that the participation of, or at least some cooperation of the parents is essential in treating young children. We certainly feel it is desirable. However, the children of unavailable parents are perhaps the neediest group of youngsters in the entire population. Can one ignore their need, or should the clinician and staff accept the responsibility of functioning as a core person for this kind of child, giving him the needed relationship with a restitutive adult? Since the child is in the day care center for sometimes as many as forty to fifty hours a week, one can postulate that the creation of a therapeutically effective program would certainly foster growth.

Since it is often difficult to separate the educational and clinical needs of such young children, this age group clearly calls for specialized staff, such as teacher–therapists, who could combine both the educational and therapeutic needs of the child.

Nursery school teachers are well–suited for the group treatment of preschool children. They are more available, are well-versed in dealing with this age group, and they use many techniques which are essentially therapeutic, though not labeled as such. Teaching and treating four and five year olds have very much in common. It is this similarity that allows a nursery school teacher to develop more easily into this kind of therapist (Schachter and Wolitzky, 1965).

The regular nursery school teacher in the day care center should be an integral part of the program plan. Her involvement extends the therapeutic process throughout the whole day instead of isolating treatment to the, let us say, two weekly sessions. It also deepens her understanding of the behavior of the children in her classroom who are not receiving special help.

The children who were helped in our program can relate better to peers and adults, have more control over their impulses, have improved language development, are friendlier and more trusting, and are more accessible to learning. Objective evaluation of the program showed that the TNG children made significant gains. The data suggested that the TNG children learned to cope better, to interact more appropriately with their environment, and to function at a higher cognitive level than had previously been the case (Holmes, 1969). The most significant change was the development of a positive sense of self. Some children's problems were so severe that this program could only make minimal inroads on their pathology. Although many of them could use intensive treatment to reach and rectify core problems, we feel that, in spite of the limitation, this type of group treatment promotes children's growth at a critical age.

We do not wish to convey the impression that there is a magic formula in working with young children, but rather that an attitude of concern and understanding of the individual child's unique development is necessary. Perhaps this book will give some impetus to aiding children. We hope that therapeutic nursery groups will become an ongoing service in all day care centers. We also hope that teachers of all young children will enjoy this book, raise questions about it, and evolve their own imaginative approaches.

References

Atkin, Edith, and Schulman, Rena, "Population Study of a Day Care Center." Mimeographed. New York: Child Development Center, 1967.

Alpert, Augusta, "A Special Therapeutic Technique for Prelatency Children with a History of Deficiency in Maternal Care." *American Journal of Orthopsychiatry* 33(1963): 161-182.

———, "The Treatment of Emotionally Distrubed Children in a Therapeutic Nursery." *American Journal of Orthopsychiatry* 25(1955): 826-834.

Axline, Virginia M., *Dibs: In Search of Self.* Boston: Houghton Mifflin Co., 1965.

Bettelheim, Bruno, *Children of the Dream.* London: Collier Macmillan Ltd., 1969.

Biber, Barbara, and Snyder, Agnes, "How Do We Know a Good Teacher." New York: Bank Street Publications, 1965.

Caplan, Gerald, *Prevention of Mental Health Disorders in Children.* New York: Basic Books, Inc., 1961.
————, *Emotional Problems of Early Childhood.* New York: Basic Books, Inc., 1955.

Erikson, Erik, *Childhood and Society.* 2d rev. ed. New York: W. W. Norton & Co., Inc., 1963.
Escalona, Sibylle, *The Roots of Individuality: Normal Patterns of Development in Infancy.* Chicago: Aldine Publishing Co., 1968.

Fenichel, Carl, "Psycho–Educational Approaches for Seriously Disturbed Children in the Classroom." *Conflict in the Classroom.* Edited by William C. Moss; Nicholas J. Long; and Ruth G. Newman. 2d rev. ed. Belmont: Wadsworth Publishing Co., 1971.
Fraiberg, Selma H., *The Magic Years: Understanding and Handling the Problems of Early Childhood.* New York: Charles Scribner's Sons, 1959.
Freud, Anna, *Normality and Pathology in Childhood: Assessment of Development.* New York: International Universities Press, Inc., 1965.
Furman, Robert A., and Katan, Anny, eds., *The Therapeutic Nursery School: A Contribution to the Study and Treatment of Emotional Disturbances in Young Children.* New York: International Universities Press, Inc., 1969.

Ginott, Haim G., *Group Psychotherapy with Children: The Theory and Practice of Play–Therapy.* New York: McGraw–Hill Book Co., Inc., 1961.
Goldfarb, William; Mintz, Irving; and Stroock, Katherine W., *A Time to Heal: Corrective Socialization: A Treatment Approach to Childhood Schizophrenia.* New York: International Universities Press, Inc., 1969.

Hartley, Ruth; Frank, Lawrence; and Goldensohn, Robert, *Understanding Children's Play.* New York: Columbia University Press, 1952.
Holmes, Douglas, and Kestenbaum, Clarice, "Evaluation of a Therapeutic Nursery Group." Mimeographed. New York: Hudson Guild Counseling Service, 1969.

Kohn, Martin, "The Adult Who Understands Him." In *The Child and the City,* pp. 45-53. New York: Day Care Council of New York, Inc., 1967.

Kohn, Martin, and Rosman, Bernice L., "Therapeutic Intervention with Disturbed Children in Day Care: Implications of the Deprivation Hypotheses." *Journal of Child Care Quarterly* 1(1971): 21-46.

Kohn, Martin, and Rudnick, Marian, "Individualized Teaching with Therapeutic Aims: A Methodological Study." *Genetic Psychology Monographs* 72(1965): 91-137.

Lambert, Ann, and Schoor, Frances, "Modified Activity Group Psychotherapy with Mixed Group of Four- and Five-Year-Old Children." Paper read January 25, 1958, at the Fifteenth Annual American Group Psychotherapy Association. Mimeographed.

Lambert, Ann; Mahler, Margaret S.; and Moore, Virginia, "A Settlement House Approach to Community Mental Health." Public Health Reports 74(1959): 957-964.

Liff, Zanvel, "An Approach to Preventive Mental Health Through the Therapeutic Nursery Group." Mimeographed. New York: Hudson Guild Counseling Service, 1962.

Mahler, Margret S., and Furer, Manuel, *Infantile Psychosis.* On Human Symbiosis and the Vicissitudes of Individuation, vol. 1. New York: International Universities Press, Inc., 1968.

Malone, Charles A., "Safety First: Comments on the Influence of External Danger in the Lives of Children of Disorganized Families." *American Journal of Orthopsychiatry* 36(1966): 3-12.

Malone, Charles A.; Pavensted, Eleanor; Mattick, Ilse; Bandler, Louise S.; Stein, Maurice R.; and Mintz, Norbett, *The Drifters: Children of Disorganized Lower Class Families.* Boston: Little, Brown and Co., 1967.

Mattick, Ilse, "Adaptation of Nursery School Techniques to Deprived Children." *Journal of the American Academy of Child Psychiatry* 4(1965): 670-700.

Moustakas, Clark E., *Children in Play Therapy.* New York: McGraw–Hill Book Co., Inc., 1953.

Murphy, Lois B., *Personality in Young Children*. Methods for the Study of Personality, vol. 1. New York: Basic Books, Inc., 1956.

————, *Widening World of Childhood: Paths Toward Mastery*. New York: Basic Books, Inc., 1962.

Read, Katherine H., *The Nursery School: A Human Relations Laboratory*. 4th ed. rev., Philadelphia: W. B. Saunders Co., 1966.

Schachter, Sherman O., and Wolitzky, David, "A Therapeutic Nursery Group in a Settlement House." *Science and Psychoanalysis* 3(1965): 225-232.

Slavson, S. R., *Analytic Group Psychotherapy with Children, Adolescents, and Adults*. New York: Columbia University Press, 1950.

Speers, Rex W., and Lansing, Cornelius, *Group Therapy in Childhood Psychosis*. Chapel Hill: University of North Carolina Press, 1965.

Wolfson, Eva, and Silverman, Martin A., "The Use of Small Educational Therapeutic Groups in a Program for Disadvantaged Preschoolers." *Journal of Jewish Board of Guardians* 1(1970): 47-59.

Wolitzky, David, "The Therapeutic Nursery Group: A Preventive Approach to Mental Health." Mimeographed. New York: Hudson Guild Counseling Service, 1962.

Children's Books in the Therapeutic Nursery Group Room

Haas, Dorothy, *Maria: Everyone Has a Name*. Racine: Western Publishing Co., 1966.

Miles, Betty, *A House for Everyone*. New York: Alfred A. Knopf, 1958.

Rey, H. A., *Curious George*. Boston: Houghton Mifflin Co., 1947.

Scott, Ann Herbert, *Sam*. New York: McGraw–Hill Book Co., Inc., 1967.

Witte, Pat, and Witte, Eve, *Who Lives Here?* New York: Western Publishing Co., 1970.

Index